STICK HOUSES

AMERICAN INDIAN STUDIES SERIES

Jill Doerfler, *Series Editor*

For a full list of titles published in this series, see the back of this book.

stories

STICK HOUSES

Matthew L. M. Fletcher

MICHIGAN STATE UNIVERSITY PRESS | East Lansing

Michigan State University Press
East Lansing, Michigan 48823-5245

Library of Congress Cataloging-in-Publication Data
Names: Fletcher, Matthew L. M., author.
Title: Stick houses : stories / Matthew L.M. Fletcher.
Description: East Lansing : Michigan State University Press, 2025. | Series: American Indian studies series
Identifiers: LCCN 2024020995 | ISBN 9781611865226 (cloth) | ISBN 9781611865233 (paperback) |
ISBN 9781609177768 (pdf) | ISBN 9781628955408 (epub)
Subjects: LCGFT: Short stories.
Classification: LCC PS3606.L4863 S75 2025 | DDC 813/.6—dc23/eng/20240506
LC record available at https://lccn.loc.gov/2024020995

Cover design by Erin Kirk
Cover art is *Metaphor*, by Jonathan Thunder

Visit Michigan State University Press at www.msupress.org

Contents

Preface

My mother, June Mamagona Fletcher, once complained to me about researchers asking her what kind of homes the Anishinaabeg of lower Michigan resided in. They wanted her to answer wigwams or teepees, some sort of traditional lodge made of materials like birch bark and clay. She would tell them every time that her ancestors lived in stick houses, going as far back as she knew, which was deep into the nineteenth century. She complained because these researchers didn't believe her, insisting that Indians didn't live in stick houses back then and that she must be wrong or lying. Indians living in stick houses didn't fit a narrative these researchers wanted to believe, it would appear.

When I was younger, my mom and I would visit my grandmother's sister, our aunt, Mary Church. She lived in the country, out past Dorr and Hopkins, Michigan. Gun Lake Potawatomi country. Right down the road from Aunt Mary's house, maybe a mile or so, was the house my grandmother, Laura Mamagona (née Pokagon/Stevens), was born in, back in 1921. Stick houses.

My grandfather, Dave Mamagona, grew up in Indian town near Kewadin, Michigan. Grand Traverse Band Odawa country. His family owned a farm on a fee allotment acquired in the nineteenth century, one of the few Odawaag able to hold onto an allotment. They sold the farm in the 1950s or so. My Aunt Gladys used the proceeds to buy a place near

Hopkins, Michigan, with her husband Lew Church, who was Potawatomi. More stick houses.

My relatives lived through administrative termination, a legal term of art of that means the federal government illegally severed ties with the lower Michigan Odawa and Potawatomi tribal nations. My tribal nations never had the benefit of the reservation land base promised in multiple treaties dating back to the early 1800s, at least under federal recognition in the 1980s and 1990s. If they were going to survive, they had to acquire land somehow and hold on to it. If they hadn't done that, there would be no me or my brother Zeke, or our own children or any of our cousins and their children.

It wasn't easy. After my great-grandmother walked on, my grandmother's siblings went to Mount Pleasant Indian Industrial Boarding School. My grandmother was denied entrance there, probably because she tested positive for tuberculosis. She spent many of her teenage years in a sanitarium in Kalamazoo, Michigan, not far from the estate promised to Match-E-Be-Nash-She-Wish (Bad Bird), the ogemaa of the Gun Lake Potawatomi tribal nation. Eventually, when she was about seventeen, her father came and got her (my mother's words, sounds like a prison escape), so she could help him raise the children he had with his second wife. She took care of those kiddos in the best way imaginable. But you know, my lovely wife, Wenona, discovered in the National Archives at Chicago that the State of Michigan used to send over people to check in on them. They wrote reports that are in the archive. They described how Laura kept the place clean, kept the kids healthy, and where the family kept its Bibles and portraits of Jesus. I can't help thinking that if one of those social workers showed up when Laura was having a bad day or was out shopping for groceries that her half-siblings would have been rounded up and shipped off to boarding school or foster care. Administrative termination didn't prevent any of the evils of colonialism; it just denied the meager benefits of federal supervision. These Indians were still wards of the government even without federal recognition. That was the way it was.

Even so, my relatives bucked the stereotype of downtrodden Indians that researchers expect to see. The Mamagona boys from Kewadin weren't supposed to go to college at the University of Michigan, but they did. My grandfather wasn't supposed to get a degree in engineering and develop clutches for the Ford Mustang, but he did. My mom and her cousins on the Church side from Hopkins weren't supposed to go to college, either, but they did. By the time my generation came along, it was expected that we would go to college. And we did.

These stories are inspired by the family's experiences and my own experiences. There's a truck stop outside of Grand Forks, North Dakota, I remember from my years as a law prof. at the University of North Dakota. When Wenona was pregnant with our first son, she liked to go there to eat and work. My high school baseball team did have Indians on it; we did get bullied by other schools, and there were fights. There really is a road in northern Michigan called Badder Road, but I don't know anyone who lives there. I've lived in Ann Arbor, Seattle, Tucson, Hoopa, and Suttons Bay (near Peshawbestown, the center of the universe). These stories are all fictional, sometimes bordering on science fiction or fantasy, but much of what goes on in this collection happened to me or someone I know. Even the cult-like chain barbecue workers chanting before a shift in an Ann Arbor alley? That happened. Singel will vouch for me on that. She was there. She was always there. Even when she wasn't.

Miigwetch.
Matthew Fletcher

Truck Stop

George glanced around the restaurant. It was cavernous, with the tables empty and set far apart from each other. Otherwise, it looked like any old diner, except that it still had telephones without dialers in the booths. He was tempted to fiddle with the phone while he waited, so see what it would call if he picked it up. He remembered eating with Stella at a truck stop once, when they were going together. He sucked in his gut a little on reflex, knowing that what he was about to eat wasn't going anywhere for a while. Thirty-eight. Christ. George figured the sole thing that kept his fat, aging, weak body alive was that he stopped smoking before it could take hold. With all the traveling, the eating processed fatty foods, the high stress levels, the extra forty pounds he carried around his waist, lack of exercise, loneliness—he wouldn't last beyond fifty. Was that self-pity? Was it self-pity that drove him to find his daughter? Is that what he doing in Grand Forks, North Dakota, watching the snow blow like a white sheet over the I-29 highway embankment? He looked around the diner again to see if she had arrived yet, if it was her this time. He wasn't the only patron. There were two old women at the other side of the restaurant, smoking and drinking coffee while they talked. He wanted to know if they were talking about him and assumed they were, the old Peshawbestown instincts dying hard. He remembered Stella offering him a cigarette in the other diner long ago. He coughed and knew in that instant he'd die coughing if he kept smoking those things.

Stella.

George knew Stella growing up in Traverse City. She was ten, fifteen years older. He never knew how old she was, but she may have even babysat him a time or two. She seemed young and came to all the young people's parties in Traverse and Peshawbestown. Maybe she seemed young because she didn't have kids and she was the youngest in her family. All her sisters were married, divorced, driving kids around, looking harried, but she always had a smile on her face. She even exercised a little, a decade before it was fashionable for 'Nishinaabes to hit the gym. George knew Stella from around, but they weren't normal friends, just acquaintances from P-Town, each with great-aunties or a grandmother living by the bay. They ran with crews that overlapped a little, so they'd visit at someone's bonfire in the woods, then maybe see each other at church the next day.

At the party his cousins threw when George got his letter of acceptance from Michigan, that's where it happened. Everyone was drinking to George, passing around cans of Old Mil and Bud Lite, laughing and giggling and picking fights to hammer out later. George already had a girlfriend, one of the other great educational hopes for the community, but they didn't like each other. They came together out of deference to everyone's expectations—they were the only smart people, so they had to go together. Stacy liked country music, Garth Brooks–type pop, but George preferred Bob Seger's "Hollywood Nights," with a smidgen of the Stooges thrown in. He was born and bred to move to Ann Arbor to walk in the footsteps of his music idols. And Stella was the one who put in the rock 'n' roll on the stereo that night. It was Patti Smith's "Horses." And no one was listening to Patti Smith in northwest lower Michigan in December 1985 except Stella and George.

They dated for a few months, trying to see how long they could keep it quiet. It turned out Stella's sister saw her in mid-January coming out of the c-store just outside of Suttons Bay with a package of tobacco, some papers, and a deluxe box of rubbers. No one ever acknowledged to their faces they suspected or knew, but there was no such thing as a false rumor in P-Town, or any small town. Maybe their peers thought they were great together, young George and old Stella, a controversy, a forbidden love story with a twist of prurient interest, but his mom and gram wouldn't stop the complaining about her. Stella, the one who knew better, the cradle-robber, took it the hardest. Some people were talking about calling the cops, not meaning it because, hell, the cops already knew. They weren't stupid.

"Maybe I just needed a reason to leave this place," she said to him the last time they were together.

George was too young to understand. "What do you mean?"

"I don't want to be one of those Indians that never leaves, that never gets out and takes a look around the world. All my uncles went to war. They saw the world. I don't want to be like those women around here that never did anything."

George's eyes teared up, despite his efforts at maturity. He cried too easily.

Stella pretended not to notice, but it confirmed that she was right. Exile was her road. "Look me up when you're rich and famous."

George let her go after that last night. He didn't know about his daughter for decades. Stella didn't tell him the night their daughter was conceived, but he liked to think it was that last night. He didn't keep his promise to look up Stella after graduation, even when he graduated from law school, but he heard little things about her when he went home visiting. No one ever said anything to him about her outright, but he thought they'd raise their voices a little when they talked about her. She was in Tucson for a while, and then she married a Hupa guy. No, it was a Ho-Chunk guy, one of those big Winnebagos. Or she was a waitress in Albuquerque at one of the Indian bars. The she married a lawyer in Minneapolis. Nothing George heard made any sense, so he wanted to ignore the news, but he couldn't stop from hanging on every word. He knew Stella called her grandmother often, but she wasn't talking about her favorite granddaughter to anyone. All that time, George knew better than to ask.

At the diner, George calculated that it had been a year and a half or so since Stella called him up. "Got your phone number off the law firm website," she said. She was calling from Eureka, California.

George told her he always hoped she would find him.

"Bullshit," she said, a little harsher than she meant. "Best thing I ever did for you was hit the road."

George couldn't disagree. "Where'd you go?"

"Nuff about me. We have to talk about your daughter."

Since Stella wouldn't say anything over the phone, George took the next flight from DC with 37,500 of his frequent-flyer miles. When he reached the Arcata-Eureka airport, he found out she was too sick to pick him up at the airport. Stomach cancer, already spread to the lymph nodes.

Stella gave birth in late August 1986, a few days before George moved into East Quad in Ann Arbor. She was at the IHS hospital in Albuquerque and broke. She hadn't eaten in a couple days. The baby was malnourished and sick—and so was the momma. The doctors and nurses took the little one away, and Stella didn't see her for a week. After they discharged Stella, she started drinking.

"I want you to know I wasn't drinking at all after I found out I was pregnant," she said with a fire in her eyes that made George want to believe her.

Stella hooked up with a big Tewa guy, who had just dropped out of college. He had sad eyes, a round face, messy hair, and he liked the way she looked in a miniskirt. He had a nice place all to himself, too. He was a good father for a few years, but wasn't someone who could take long-term responsibility for a sickly Indian baby.

"They came for our daughter right after that," she said. "Our daughter," she repeated. "I'm not used to saying that. She was five."

Stella didn't know where they took her. "I think you should find her. I named her after my grandmother, but her adoptive parents would have changed it." George said it wouldn't make sense to change the name of a five-year-old, but Stella told him, like she used to, to shut up and quit arguing with her. She died a month later, after George had already met one of the false candidates.

He called them the false candidates in an attempt to make it sound like he was certain they weren't his children, but he never really was sure. It disturbed him how many Indian babies disappeared into white society without a trace. The Indian Child Welfare Act was a joke. He took Stella's charge with a degree of seriousness he never gave to his job with Goldman Petoskey. He followed every lead he could and used up his 250,000 frequent-flyer miles in the first four months. He met five Indian women in five different states. There was at least one thing about their stories that wouldn't jive, such as the state of adoption (Nebraska instead of New Mexico, for instance) or the name on the birth certificate. And George was a stickler for paperwork. But what mattered, he knew, was what he saw when he looked into their eyes. And he didn't see anything in these young women. Nothing he recognized. He wondered if he had been away from Peshawbestown and his family for so long, he couldn't recognize a 'Nishinaabe if he saw one.

Five false candidates so far.

George was on his second cup of coffee, thinking he was being stood up, when his sixth candidate walked in. She was bundled in every conceivable layer of warm clothing, and he couldn't see her face. She was tall and carried a backpack, old army surplus. She stomped her boots on the rug and shook off the snow as best as she could. He was the only one sitting alone, so she looked right at him for a moment before beginning to unwrap. She took off her scarves, hat, and gloves and walked over to his table.

George knew that this young woman was his daughter in Joan Didion's ordinary instant. She looked like his own mother did in a picture he kept, one where his mom is laughing outside the cider mill in Antrim County. His mom at twenty-two looked like this woman. Long, black, and straight hair. Round face, like the moon. Narrow eyes that made people mistake her for Asian when she was younger. And tall. Mamagona women tended to grow like weeds.

"George Mamagona?" she said, pronouncing his last name like they used to say his grandmother's name down at the Vets, with the "ma'am" at the beginning instead of the "mom."

He stood and shook her hands, unable to say anything. He swallowed hard and motioned for the woman to sit down. She still wore a massive winter coat, and it took some doing to get it off. He heard the static crackle as the coat released her hair and cringed. He knew the feeling and smiled. The god-awful static electricity of dry winters would be their first commonality.

Since he didn't say anything, she stuck out her hand and said, "Lisa Hyde." They zapped each other as they touched.

George had emailed Lisa a few weeks earlier on her UND student account. He worried about sounding like a stalker or a predator when he first contacted the candidates. Lisa didn't respond for a week. George was about to call information when his computer bleeped with her response. This Lisa had talked it over with her friends and family. She'd be willing to meet him on the off chance he was the real deal. There was a truck stop on the west side of I-29 in Grand Forks. She said the food there was good, and no one from the university ate over there. It wouldn't be suspicious. It would be neutral and safe. It was quiet.

Lisa was just a little older than George was when he dated Stella and became a father.

"You don't look like your picture," she said. She kept a poker face, making clear her mistrust, puffing up her worldly experience.

It was true. "I've gained a little weight since that picture was taken," he said. "And a few gray hairs, I suppose." He was twenty-six when they took the picture. His suits hadn't gone out of style yet, he hoped.

"So what makes you think you're my father?"

Your eyes, squinting, like my mother when she's angry. And your hair, the exact shade as my mother's hair before I was born.

"Paperwork," he said, saying the wrong thing like a cold-hearted bastard and wondering how he would recover.

"Oh, yeah?" She looked at the exit on the far side of the restaurant. He was losing her. He wished he brought the photograph of his mother at the cider mill.

"Well, that's the way it's done." What the hell did that mean?

Lisa narrowed her eyes again and that time he saw his grandmother. She used to hit her grandchildren with a flyswatter when they got into things or made too much of a racket. Lisa looked restless.

George looked around for the server, thinking that if they ordered some food, Lisa would stay. The server was talking to the old women and didn't see him.

Lisa noticed and said, "It's because we're Indian."

George laughed out loud. He'd heard that before. "That's what my gram used to say in restaurants. Always picking for a fight, I think. I thought you said you came in here a lot."

"I do. By myself. I bring another Indian, maybe she gets nervous. One Indian is okay. Two is a tribe, as Sherman Alexie says," she muttered.

George laughed. He liked this woman, his daughter. All he had to do was convince her. "I think you're my daughter," he said.

"Really, how do you know for sure?" Lisa was all business. He wondered if she had done this before. Had she looked for him? Had she looked for Stella? She crossed her arms and looked right into his eyes, a challenge from an Indian if there ever was one. In that gesture, he saw Stella and, again, almost wept.

"I told you," he said, choking a little, looking for breathing room. "I have a copy of your birth certificate." It was a lie, in part. He had copies of several birth certificates of other candidates. Any of them could have been his daughter. There was just no way for him to be certain—on paper.

The server came over and asked Lisa if she wanted something to drink to start. Lisa asked for a glass of water and a hot tea. She told the server she was ready to order, too, and asked for a veggie omelet. George took the time to compose himself and ordered a cheeseburger with fries. He wanted them crispy, he said. A high-maintenance lawyer.

After the server walked away, they were silent for a time. George wasn't sure how to talk to his daughter. He knew he couldn't just blurt out that Lisa looked like his mother, grandmother, and his former lover all in one. It was true, it seemed, but he knew this woman sitting before him wouldn't be buying that particular brand of bullshit.

Lisa broke the silence. "So what kind of law do you practice?"

George felt relieved by the change in subject. "Indian law."

"No duh?" Sarcasm and a little impatience. Raised eyebrows.

"Sorry. I do a little lobbying, some employment and labor law for tribal casinos. Tax and gaming compact negotiations. I travel a lot. Sacramento. Omaha. LA. Phoenix. Minneapolis. I live in DC. Well, Arlington, actually."

"Ever been to Grand Forks?"

"Nope. Well, maybe I drove through once on the interstate going east–west. It seemed like the state that just never ended."

Lisa smiled, underreacting to his little joke.

"You from here?"

"Minot," she said. "I was an air-force brat."

George searched his mind. "Never heard of Minot." None of the North Dakota tribes needed to hire a DC lobbying firm. He paused and glanced outside. "So you're used to this weather?" The weather channel had told him it was 26 degrees below zero that morning. With the wind chill, fifty below. Outside, with his nerves working, he had never felt colder in his life.

"Not really." She had stopped staring at him but seemed resigned to something, something like failure.

Why couldn't George think of anything that would convince her?

"What do you remember about your mother?" he asked, hoping to find a hook in there somewhere.

"Not a bit," she said. But she was interested in what he would have to say next.

George knew this was the make-or-break moment. "She was older than I was, you know. Her name was Stella Pigeon." He closed his eyes to remember her. "She liked Patti Smith's poetry. We'd talk about what the poems meant and disagreed on everything. She'd always tell me not to argue with her about Patti Smith. Her favorite movie was *Jeremiah Johnson*. Her favorite color was blue. She drove a Honda motorcycle in the summer, and she drove fast." He opened his eyes. Lisa was paying close attention.

"She named you after her grandmother. Emily."

The name Emily seemed to have no impact, but George suspected that this woman sitting across from him was trying hard not to give anything away. He searched her eyes, looking for something. He was close to crying again. What did he have to do?

And then Lisa's mobile rang to the tune of a Patti Smith song. One of the new ones. He apologized and fumbled in her coat for the phone.

George said, "I didn't know you could buy a Patti Smith ringtone."

Lisa smiled at him as she found the phone. She turned away and looked outside as she spoke. "Hello?"

There were too many coincidences for George to be wrong. He knew now that this woman was his daughter. The paperwork suggested it, the facts were consistent, and the way this was happening—the smiles, the looks, the gestures, Patti Smith—it all fit. Or did it? This woman was his last lead, he had to admit. After Lisa, there were no other candidates to hunt down. He was desperate and down to his last out.

"What's the problem?" Lisa said. "If he won't eat, then tell him no Pooh Bear book when I get home." Pause. "OK." A long pause. "No, put him on. I'll tell him."

George stared at the floor, trying to think of what to say next. The server arrived with their meals. George thanked her. He looked back at Lisa to see her staring back at him, still on the phone. He knew she was working on it in her mind, trying to decide whether to take a chance with him, forgive him, trust him, accept him into her own family. There was a part of him that didn't want her to believe right away, to make him work for it. He wanted the long pursuit before the inevitable moment when she began to believe. Maybe it would take a week. A month. A year, with several visits? Piles of documentation? Photographs? The objective evidence was there already, but the subjective, the emotional, proof required more. Perhaps shared experiences. Would this moment in this diner be enough? Had they shared enough? Had they shared anything?

"Hi, baby," she said into the phone, gentler this time. "I love you," she said. And when she heard a tiny response, she glowed. She looked back at George, holding the phone away from her ear.

George thought, if I were her, would I believe?

Lisa smiled at him for a long, long time before she pointed to her mobile. "Want to meet your grandson?"

Knuckle-Curve

Mike gripped the baseball and paced the mound. The ball was scuffed and dirty, six-and-a-half innings old. They only rubbed down four baseballs before the game for Michigan high school games. He paused long enough to bring Vanderkolb, the big senior first baseman, out to the mound.

"Wassup, hoss?"

Vanderkolb was a football player slumming in the spring with the baseball team for kicks. He was a tall and powerful quarterback, who had gone undefeated in his two years as a starter for South Christian High School.

"I'm fine," Mike said. He wasn't fine. He was upset. He looked over at the bench and saw Coach Kooiker with his foot on the top step, examining his star pitcher with squinted eyes.

"You tired or what, hoss?" Vanderkolb asked.

Mike didn't enjoy being called "hoss." He never wanted to be a jock for South. He wasn't a wide receiver or a linebacker or a tackle like so many of his teammates. His catcher, DeKonig, was a tackle who would play for Eastern Michigan in the fall. Eddings, the burly third baseman, was a linebacker and would join Vanderkolb at Michigan State. Williams and VanderKodde, his speedy outfielders, were underclass speedsters, who had caught so many of Vanderkolb's bullets for scores. South Christian was a football school—winning four of the last eight state championships—that used its football talent to power the baseball team on the side. Mike never played football. He was a pitcher, not a gorilla.

Mike scowled at Vanderkolb, a scowl born more from personal animus than competitive fire. "Get out of here." He was tired of being bossed around by the pimply quarterback, who took it upon himself to be everyone's leader. He disliked Vanderkolb—and most of the rest of his teammates, for that matter. He often sat in the dugout on days he didn't pitch, hoping the team would lose.

On more than one occasion, he found himself wishing for a serious injury to befall Vanderkolb. Something in his throwing shoulder maybe.

Vanderkolb took Mike's scowl as a good sign and bounded back to his position.

Mike had an 8-1 lead going into the bottom of the seventh and final inning. He had already struck out thirteen Wayland hitters, a typically dominant performance for him. The only run was unearned, thanks to an uncharacteristic throwing error by Jim DeKuiper at short. He toed the rubber and looked in. Steve McNeese, Wayland's sophomore center fielder, was up. He had struck McNeese out twice already. Fastball sign.

Mike went into his windup and snapped off a heater at McNeese's knees. That one felt great. He knew the scouts sitting behind the backstop with their portable radar guns would see that he was throwing harder in the later innings than in the early innings, getting stronger as the game wore on. Two more fastballs at the letters and McNeese sat down, completely outmatched.

Pitching against Wayland meant that Mike would be trying to retire his close friends. He grew up in Wayland, going to Steeby Elementary and the Pearl Street middle school with half the players on the other side of the field. However, like so many of Wayland's promising male athletes, he attended South Christian, fifteen miles north of Wayland in Cutlerville, a Grand Rapids suburb.

Preston Brown stepped to the plate. Mike had known Preston since first grade. Until ninth grade, Mike, Preston, and Kevin Sessler had played ball together every summer, three Indian boys with talent and baseball flowing through their veins every day of the year. They had lost only two or three games in seven years, dominating Allegan County grade-school summer baseball. In eighth grade, they were the student managers for

Coach Pokagon's 1986 varsity team, which had reached the regional finals, the state's final eight. The rest of that summer, they played American Legion ball and talked about winning a state championship for Wayland.

Instead, Mike's dad forced him north to a sports-fanatical parochial school with no hot lunches and no busing. Mike's dad had dreamed of playing professional ball, but he could never hit a curve ball. He gave up baseball, married a Potawatomi woman, and took a job in construction. He pushed his son hard, and he lived vicariously through the boy.

Wayland and South played in the same league, so Mike faced Wayland frequently. In three years on the South varsity, he had confronted and beaten Wayland six times. That day would be the seventh and last time. Because South was only a few miles north, the games between them—baseball, football, softball, boys and girls basketball, volleyball—could be brutal. But South was a powerhouse and towered above Wayland.

Mike threw a fastball at Preston's knees for strike one—Preston always took strike one. Mike wondered if the pitch registered ninety on any of the three radar guns behind home plate. Preston stepped out of the box, smiling like he knew he would smack the next pitch over the scoreboard beyond the left-field fence. Mike had told his friend more than once that he was the high-school equivalent of the Mike Hargrove–style human rain delay.

Preston was born to play ball for Coach Pokagon, his uncle. Coach Pokagon was a big Potawatomi guy, who once drove a ball to the wall off of Dave Rozema during tryouts for the Grand Rapids J.C. team a few days before Rozema signed with the Tigers in the 1970s. Preston had been going to Wayland baseball games since he was seven, when his uncle, an English teacher, took over the team. During Coach Pokagon's tenure, Wayland's teams were always in the top half of the league and made a deep run into the state tournament every few years.

Preston had been crushed when Mike said he would be going to South. They both knew Wayland wouldn't have a good chance of doing any damage in the state tournament without Mike's fastball. Preston had actually challenged Mike to a fight but instead broke down into adolescent tears. He made Mike promise never to tell anyone about the crying.

Preston returned to the box and settled in. Mike knew Preston was a right-handed, dead-pull hitter who could drive a fastball up and over the plate to the gap, so he threw the slurve thing he'd been throwing since the summer after fourth grade in neighborhood whiffle ball tournaments, the one that started at the batter's head and broke down on the inside corner. Preston knew what was coming from the way Mike grunted and where the ball was headed—he'd seen Mike do the same thing for almost a decade—and waited on the pitch. He took a beautiful cut—probably the best cut he would ever take at a breaking pitch in his life, the same cut he'd been taking in hundreds of whiffle ball games for years—and fouled the pitch off down the left-field line. With a taped-up wooden broom handle or a plastic bat, he would have taken the pitch inside-out to right field for a hit, but he had never acquired the strength or timing to do it with a thirty-ounce aluminum bat and a live baseball.

Preston walked back to the plate from halfway down the first base line, still smiling but looking a little desperate. Mike knew his friend's best chance to get a hit off him was gone. He wouldn't make contact with another of Mike's pitches. Mike had faced Preston nineteen times in high school games and had struck him out eleven times, popped him up four times, forced three weak grounders, and plunked him in the armpit once—the first time they had faced each other, almost laughing too hard to play.

For both teams, that day's game was the final game of the regular season. Mike watched Preston milk his last at-bat for everything he could. Preston's baseball career would be over in a few days or weeks, but Mike's career was just beginning. Mike would decide after the season whether to take the scholarship with the University of Michigan or sign with the Phillies scout, sitting behind the backstop, chain-smoking cigarettes and telling bad jokes and making promises to Mike's father. Preston had already decided to go to Notre Dame on an academic scholarship.

Preston picked up his bat, bending his stout frame like an old man. He squeezed it and looked like he was going to step back in for another pitch when, like an afterthought, he licked the tip of his finger and held it aloft, signaling in their ancient language that the wind was blowing out and he was about to take Mike deep. Mike chuckled in spite of himself, and he could hear Kevin in the dugout laughing out loud at the private joke. A couple of the other guys in the Wayland dugout tittered because they knew the joke, too, from the summer days of whiffle ball in Preston's backyard.

Mike threw the 0-2 pitch at Preston's eyes to see if he would bite. The hitter let it go by and stepped back out of the box.

Mike wiped the sweat off his forehead and looked over at the Wayland dugout. He wondered what it would have been like if he had stayed at Wayland. Would he be out there facing Vanderkolb with a 2-1 lead, hoping to keep the muscular power hitter in the park and preserve the lead? Would Wayland be 25-4 like South instead of 17-12 coming in? Would any of the scouts sitting behind home be there to watch him? Wayland had no sports legacy. He remembered Preston telling him about the seniors from two years earlier, who cried like babies in the dugout after the game near the end of the year that guaranteed them a winning season. For these seniors, who had played basketball and football and baseball, it was the first time they had ever recorded a winning record in any sport in high school.

Then Mike heard Coach Pokagon's deep growl rumble out from the third base coach's box. "Get back in there, Brown. It's getting dark."

It was getting dark, and the wind was picking up, blowing out to right field. It would rain hard right after the game ended.

Mike saw Preston's mom leaning on the fence down the left field side beyond the dugout, pointing her 35-millimeter camera at her son. He saw Preston's dad training a camcorder toward home plate from behind the backstop. They went to every one of Preston's games. They had even traveled to Battle Creek the year before when Mike pitched for South in the state semifinals against Harper Creek.

Preston heeded his uncle and stepped back in. He wasn't smiling anymore; he was trying to survive for a few more seconds, trying to get the bat on the ball and make something happen. Mike took the sign for another fastball and delivered. Preston took a cut, and it looked to Mike that he had just nicked it foul. DeKonig thought so too and asked the umpire for another ball. When the ump just stared at the catcher, Preston took off running to first as fast as his short little legs would allow, which wasn't very fast at all. The catcher held out his hand even as he stupidly stared at Preston before he realized the ball was in play.

The backup infielder wearing a battling helmet and coaching first for Wayland frantically waved Preston to second before DeKonig recovered the ball. There was no play at second.

Mike received the ball back from his slow-witted catcher and scowled. He looked over at Preston on second and shook his head. Preston stood there clapping his hands like a little boy, as he always did. Mike would never admit it until they were both decades older, but he envied Preston. While Mike and Kevin did roadwork and lifted free weights after school, Preston read Foucault, Emily Dickinson, and Dostoyevsky and rented imported art films from the Rite-Aid next to Harding's Market. Preston's future rested with his mind, a much more resilient organ than Mike's throwing arm or Kevin's powerful wrists and hands. A slip on wet grass during a low-key jog in the outfield could terminate their budding baseball careers. Preston would have no such worries. An injury to his chubby body would only make him a little later for class. Preston had a much better chance to become a professional writer or an Indian lawyer than Mike would have of making it to the big leagues. In fact, it was statistically probable that Mike's baseball career would be over before Preston finished graduate school.

Mike toed the rubber and heard a smattering of excitement from the Wayland dugout. The game wasn't legitimately in doubt, but Preston was only the third hitter to reach base, and he represented a second run. Mike hadn't given up more than one run in a game since the semifinal against Harper Creek the year before.

Richie Rivas came up to the plate. Along with Preston and Kevin, he was one of the three Potawatomi kids to play for Coach Pokagon. George Mamagona, the light-hitting outfielder, was the fourth Indian on the team, an Ottawa guy. Unlike the other Indian players, Richie was loud and brash, bad-tempered, and occasionally violent. His mom had died when he was young, and his dad was an alcoholic and had disappeared a few months earlier. Richie lived half the time with his older brother and the other half of the time over Coach Pokagon's garage on Maple Street.

Richie was also a fantastic athlete, loaded with speed, power, and grace, and he could dominate a baseball field, a football field, or a basketball court at any given moment. The first time Richie faced Mike, he had cranked a long homer over the plastic center field fence at South

Christian. He bragged about it endlessly but, since then, had struck out nine times in a row against Mike.

Seeing Richie was always hard on Mike because he was a long-ball threat and also because it reminded him of something his father had said. In his arguments with his dad about going to South, he complained to his dad that he didn't want to go there because it was loaded with arrogant, self-righteous Dutch Christian Reformed kids. His dad responded harshly. "Boy," he said, "you have to think about your future. Playing ball with those stinking Indians will get you nowhere. Indians like Richie."

Mike looked in, but DeKonig was standing up and the ump was calling time. Vanderkolb had trotted out to the mound.

"What?" Mike asked.

"I want you to brain this punk. He took some cheap shots at us in football, and I want you to hurt this guy."

Mike was tired of the macho crap. "No." He turned away.

Vanderkolb grabbed his shoulder. His grip was amazing and painful. Mike wondered if the quarterback could end his promising pitching prospects with one twist of his wrist. He put his nose up close to Mike's face. Mike could smell Skoal.

"I ain't askin, Singel. I want you to fuckin break this timber nigger's jaw."

Mike watched the big man return to first. The game wasn't fun anymore. He looked over at Preston, who hadn't seen anything out of the ordinary. He toed the rubber and looked in. Fastball, up and in. Jesus, everyone wanted Richie decapitated. He went into his set and checked Preston. He had his standard two-foot lead. He could have been sitting at his gram's dinner table, eating spaghetti, and reading the *Sporting News* for all the intensity on his face.

Mike's pitch headed for the outside corner, and Richie lunged for it, popping it up on the first base side. Vanderkolb drifted over and hovered below it. For an instant, Mike suspected the big man would drop the ball on purpose, but it settled into his glove. He jogged back to the mound to deliver the ball to Mike personally.

"Weak, Singel," he said.

Mike looked away.

"What did you call me?" Richie was yelling at DeKonig. "Say it again," he said. "Say it again so the ump will hear you and toss your butt out of here. I dare you."

DeKonig ignored Richie.

"Sit down, Rivas," Vanderkolb yelled from the mound.

Richie turned and looked at Vanderkolb. "Shut up," he said, "you big hick."

"Sit down, batter," the ump said. "That's enough."

Mike knew little Freddie Munsen, the second baseman, was up next, but he wasn't coming to the plate. Instead, he saw Kevin Sessler whipping around a weighted bat, warming up. Coach Pokagon had sat Kevin because he had wrenched his ankle the night before at Kenowa Hills, so he hadn't played yet.

Unlike Preston, Kevin had cut his long hair when he started basketball in ninth grade. His older brother Charles Sessler had played basketball and baseball for Wayland fifteen years before, averaging twenty points a game and hitting .375, an all-stater in both sports. The sports-mad locals referred to Kevin as "Little Sess," or "Little Sis" when he played badly. Kevin was taller and more of a rebounder and defender in hoops, so he didn't score as much as Big Sess. But in baseball, Kevin was the real deal, breaking Big Sess's RBI record the Monday before the South game. Like his older brother, Kevin was going to Western Michigan, an invited walk-on.

Mike's battles with Kevin were always exciting. Kevin only hit .250 against Mike, but his four hits were all doubles and he had driven in six against the hard-throwing righty. Scouts came to watch Kevin because of a long foul ball he had hit off one of Mike's fastballs up and in the year before in a summer league game.

It was Preston and Kevin who had gotten Mike interested in baseball way back in third grade. His own father's attempts to teach him to catch and throw never caught on. He preferred his Intellivision video game console. When Preston moved in next door, he talked Preston into coming outside, where they would get muddy climbing trees, riding their dirt bikes, and stalking each other as Cowboy and Indian. Mike started going with Preston to family picnics in Salem or Dorr. Preston's family—dozens of Anishinaabes: Ottawas, Potawatomis, and a few Chippewas—would meet and play softball and eat hot dogs and fry bread all day long. Playing ball with the Pokagons and Pigeons and Mamagonas and Churches was fun, and Mike discovered he was really good at it. He met Kevin, Richie, George, and Preston's uncle there and developed his love for the game.

Mike joined the Little League and was placed on Kevin and Preston's teams—first with Dancer's Fashions in the junior division and then with Harding's Market in the senior division. In their four years in Little League, they lost only two games and won the league every year. Ditto the Babe Ruth League playing for Wayland Standard.

Kevin dug in a little gingerly and looked up at Mike. Mike knew the scouts would be more interested in their match-up. He looked in and got the sign for a straight change. He liked DeKonig's call and moved into his delivery. As he let the ball go, he heard Eddings yell, "Going!" and knew he had forgotten about Preston completely.

Preston was slow afoot, but he took a gigantic lead to see if he could get Mike's attention, and when he didn't he took off. Kevin saw the huge jump Preston had and laid the bat on his shoulder.

DeKonig caught the ball cleanly but had to throw over a six-five batter who made no effort to move out of the way. The ball sailed and Preston slid in, well ahead of the tag.

As Eddings returned the ball to his pitcher, Coach Pokagon said to Preston, "And what the hell are you doing here?"

Preston, huffing and puffing and wiping the dust off, said, "He forgot about me."

"So what, Brown." Coach Pokagon refused to treat his nephew different than the other players. "You forgot the golden rule."

"I know—never make the first or third out at third. But he completely forgot about me. I had a great jump."

"Your run doesn't mean anything."

"Yeah, but when will I ever get a chance to steal third off a future hall-of-famer?"

"I think you're too smart for your own good, Brown."

Mike listened to the whole exchange with a great degree of envy. He couldn't ever see himself having a conversation like theirs with Coach Kooiker. And then he wondered if the scouts would make a big deal about the fact that he had let Wayland's slowest player steal third. He shook his head and tried to focus.

It wasn't hard. The three of them had been in the same situation dozens—maybe hundreds—of times before in their backyards. Preston on base. Mike pitching, facing Kevin. The fourth player—usually George or even Preston's younger brother Ed—roaming the yard, waiting to chase down the hard plastic ball covered in duct tape.

Mike worked from the windup. Coach Pokagon was right when he said the run didn't mean anything. Preston wasn't going anywhere. Kevin had been sitting on the bench all day, so DeKonig called for a high fastball.

Kevin fouled it straight back, making it 0-2.

Mike thought about throwing the knuckle-curve Kevin taught him to throw maybe six, seven years earlier. It was the most vicious pitch he had in his repertoire, but he couldn't control it. He tried throwing it in hardball practice a few years back—the first time the pitch surprised DeKonig and smashed right into his junk—but he hadn't tried it in a real game until a month earlier. He'd only throw it 0-2, nobody on, and at least a five-run lead—the situation here—or if a real hitter was up. He had struck out Berrios from Ottawa Hills and Curtis from Forest Hills Central with the pitch in the last few weeks. They'd be playing for LSU and the Florida State League, respectively, in the next year.

DeKonig called for another change, and Mike agreed. Kevin had seen it already in the at-bat—not to mention the hundreds of times he'd seen it in the backyard—and knew it would start in the left-handed batter's box and tail in to the outside corner. He waited and smacked a ferocious line drive over Vanderkolb's head that drifted just foul down the line.

The scouts were loving it.

Do I show him the knuckle-curve? Mike thought. He's never seen the real thing, only the whiffle ball version. He looked over at Preston, who was looking away toward the plate but pointing with his left hand to the knuckles on his right hand as if reading Mike's mind. Mike realized that Kevin was taking signs from Coach Pokagon but could have noticed Preston's signal. He shook his head, looked down, and smiled. He hadn't had so much fun since whiffle ball. He turned, and Vanderkolb was standing right in front of him, an angry ogre with a bad smell.

"What?" Mike said.

Vanderkolb turned away and spoke into his glove. "Throw the high heat and strike this brown piece of shit out." Then he left the mound.

Mike shook off the bigotry. Did Vanderkolb even know he was an Anishinaabe too? The last two outs had been alternately fun and horrifying. He looked around the diamond—teammates he despised, opponents he respected, scouts in the bleachers, pitching against his home team, darkness approaching, and rain coming. He decided to throw the knuckle-curve and, to his astonishment, DeKonig called for it. He saw Kevin fighting off a smile.

Kevin had saved Mike. After Mike began attending South Christian, Wayland football players and wrestlers started egging his house and setting his family's trash can on fire. It got worse right before the big football game with South but stopped altogether when Mike rode to the game with Kevin, Preston, Big Sess, and Old Man Sess. He sat on the Wayland side with his friends. He sat with what amounted to Wayland sports royalty.

Mike notched his fingernail on the ball and delivered the knuckle-curve to Kevin. Kevin had already guessed from the way Mike held the ball in his glove what the pitch would be and waited. He checked his swing because the ball dropped too sharply and hit the edge of the plate. DeKonig had trouble blocking the pitch because of an old football injury to his hip. He couldn't get his knee down fast enough. Instead of the ball bouncing off his fleshy thigh and going nowhere, it hit the hard plastic of his knee guard and shot straight back out to the mound.

Preston saw the whole thing and was waiting for a pitch in the dirt. When he saw the ball get away from DeKonig, he sprinted toward home.

Mike, surprised to see the ball back in his glove, was slow to react. He saw Preston move, so he threw the ball back to DeKonig. Too late.

Preston slid home and popped up like a jack-in-the-box. He gave Kevin a high-five, and they laughed like the whole thing was planned.

Then, for no good reason, especially given the fact that South had a six-run lead with two outs in the bottom of the final inning with no one on base, DeKonig shoved Preston in the back and sent the kid sprawling across the dirt. Kevin, utterly shocked by DeKonig's action, stared first at Preston on the ground and then at the catcher, who was smiling like a mean little boy who has pulled the wings of a fly, and he never saw Vanderkolb fly across the diamond with a bead on him. The quarterback had been waiting for something to happen and jumped on his opportunity, moving like a linebacker with amazing closing speed. Eddings, who actually was a linebacker with amazing closing speed, flew toward the melee from his third base station but was intercepted by Coach Pokagon and George Mamagona, who had rushed to his teammates' and friends' assistance.

Simultaneously, Richie Rivas leaped out the dugout and leveled DeKonig as though on a corner blitz. The catcher, screaming epithets at Kevin and Preston about drunken Indians, retarded Indians, and faggot Indians, never knew what hit him.

Coach Kooiker screamed across the diamond at Coach Pokagon to let Eddings go and exercise control over his damn players. The coach and George did everything they could to hold back Eddings, who was shouting and squirming and threatening their lives.

Richie was Vanderkolb's real target, and they squared off. Distracted by Eddings, no one noticed them at first. Richie, a veteran of more than thirty brutal fistfights with his older brother, punched Vanderkolb in the face five times before the big kid could react. He fell to the ground gushing blood from his face.

When it was over the umpires declared a forfeit, Richie was arrested, and Vanderkolb and DeKonig rode a Wayland Area Ambulance to Allegan County General Hospital.

Mike did not leave with the rest of his team. He lived only a few hundred yards away from the field, right next door to the school. He didn't speak to anyone on his way out, even when Kevin and Preston said he played a good game.

A week later Wayland's season ended when a corn-fed flamethrower from Comstock came into town and tossed a one-hitter in the pre-district qualifier. Mike pitched South Christian to the state semifinals in Battle Creek again. He pitched shutout ball for eight innings, matched by his opponent, but lost on a ninth-inning home run by an all-state quarterback from Brighton with massive forearms.

Preston, Kevin, Ed, and Preston's parents were in attendance.

After the game, they all went to Preston's house and sat around in the backyard. The grass had grown up over the base paths and the mound, but there were still deep grooves in the lawn. They talked about Little League and Babe Ruth, about how they never lost when they were all together. They talked about how Mike had learned to pitch, and Kevin had learned to hit over the years they played whiffle ball. They talked about the hundreds of games they had played, all the baseball dramas they had acted out.

Mike said that after the Wayland–South game he had wanted to quit the team and the school, but his dad talked him into finishing.

They sat in silence for several minutes. It was late, but it wouldn't be getting dark for a while.

"Let's play a game," Preston said. "One last game. Me and Ed. We'll take you guys on right now."

Mike, tired, sore, and emotionally spent, looked around at his friends and jumped up out of his lawn chair. He had been waiting for someone to say something. He went into the garage to see if his old glove—the one he always kept at Preston's house for whiffle ball—was still there. It was, hanging from the same old nail. He grabbed it and bounded into the outfield.

Badder Road

"Auto mechanic school? That's it? So they drive off into the distance on their motorcycles. They survived the reservation. They avoided the racist police. They got the girl. They learned life lessons. But all they get out of it is a free trip to auto mechanic school? That's pathetic. How come when white guys ride off into the distance on their motorcycles, they go to Harvard Law School or Europe, but when Indians ride off into the distance, they're going to auto mechanic school?"

"Or art school," Beercan said. "Sometimes they go to art school."

Ben nodded his head and raised a warm can of pop to his lips. "Yeah. Art school, too. Indians are always doing arts and crafts. How come your Pepsi Coke is always warm?"

"Electricity's out this week," Beercan said. "Probably get it turned on again in a week or so."

Ben looked around. He just realized that the room had faded to dark. The sun set a half hour earlier. The only light in the room was the residual luminosity of the early August sun hanging around late into the evening.

Beercan stood and retrieved a candle from the top of his empty, dusty bookshelf. "I'll light this, but it will just draw in the moths."

Ben watched as Beercan struck a match and held it under his open palm for a few seconds before lighting the candle. "Why do you do that? Doesn't it hurt?"

Beercan sat down and shrugged. "It's just something I do."

The house at the end of Badder Road in Kalkaska County had been in Beercan's family forever. No one ever wanted to live there. The place had been decrepit and a pit since before Beercan was born, but he lived there because he couldn't afford anywhere else. At least it was free. In the last few days, Beercan took down all the old newspaper out of the walls that had been his insulation in the winter when he learned the recycling station at the high school in Kalkaska would pay him for it. The proceeds paid for a sixer of Pepsi, but it wasn't enough to get the juice running again.

Just after Beercan popped one open and sat down to watch the light fade in his living room, Ben pulled in with his grandmother's old Escort. Ben wasn't supposed to be driving because his license was suspended, but he kept saying that he had a treaty right to drive wherever the hell he wanted.

Ben stared at the flickering candle light on Beercan's cigarette-burned coffee table. He would stay with Beercan at least a week, maybe longer. He left Indian town in Harbor Springs with less than an eighth a tank of gas, and the gauge was way past E after his trip to Badder Road.

"Your gram know you took her car?"

Ben smiled. "She never goes anywhere anyway."

Beercan shook his head. "You give us lazy, shiftless Indians a bad name."

Ben nodded. "It's true. It's all true."

"Well, while you're here, you can be the house Indian and clean up around here."

Ben looked around the old house. There wasn't much furniture except a few old couches and broken tables. Beercan didn't have any possessions so he didn't leave a mess. "Okay," Ben said.

A large gray moth exploded in a spectacular ball of flame over Beercan's coffee table.

“Shit!” Ben shouted. “You don’t see that very often.”

Beercan nodded. He saw it all the time, and it wasn’t a big deal. He knew that, if Ben stared at the candle long enough, not a whole lot would matter.

The other insects revolving around the candle flame drifted away but returned to their worship after a few seconds. It was better when they were close to light; that way, one could account for all of them.

“You still got that warrant out on you?” Ben asked. He took a pull off his second can of warm pop. The carbonation burned his throat, and he coughed before Beercan could answer. “You got anything to mix this?”

Beercan shrugged. “I don’t think you want to go into the kitchen. Besides, we quit drinkin, remember?”

“Yeah.” Ben took another quick swallow and tried to think of another way to conserve Beercan’s limited supply of pop.

“And I don’t think there was ever a warrant out for me,” Beercan said. “They just wanted to talk to me.”

“Same difference.”

“That Rodney deserved what he got anyway,” Beercan said.

“Damn right,” Ben said.

Beercan cracked the knuckles on right hand. They were still sore, and there was a small scab covering what was left of the cut he got from Rodney’s tooth.

Ben produced a smoke and lit a match.

“Put that out,” Beercan barked. “You want to start a fire in here?”

Ben looked around the room. “Didn’t you tell me you got rid of all the newspapers?”

Beercan thought about it and relaxed. “Oh, yeah. Go ahead.”

Ben lit up, took a long drag, and then let his arm dangle off the side of his armrest. The odor of the burning tobacco filled the room.

The men stared at the candle a long while, long enough for Ben’s cigarette to burn down on its own.

"How are you going to pay for the light bill?"

Beercan shrugged, still staring at the candle. "Cans on the side of the road. Been thinking about going out to tomorrow. You can come, too."

Ben shifted his butt on the loveseat. He could feel a metal spring right under the fabric of the seat cushion. "How many're you gonna need?"

"What am I? A math major? You're the one who went to college. You figure it out. Make your lazy ass self useful."

Ben coughed. The old ache in his chest was back from just one drag of a cigarette.

"What about the one they played at The Bay in Suttons Bay? The one about the gay Indian in Seattle? Didn't you used to live in Seattle?"

Ben nodded. "Yeah, for about a week. The Indians there are all snooty."

"Well, did you see the movie?"

"Yeah. I went with Tahsanchat when she was in town. She loved it. She cried at the end when they were singing 'Amazing Grace' for the dead guy."

Beercan thought about the past and smiled. "My family used to sing that all the time. They said Indians were dying all the time, so it didn't matter when you sung it."

"I don't get it. Isn't it strange Indians are always singing 'Amazing Grace'? Isn't that assimilation? What about Indian songs?"

Beercan leaned forward and looked at Ben with a crooked face, like he always did when he was about to make a point. "You know any Indian songs, cuz?"

"No."

"See? Besides, what difference does it make? You never went to church when you were a kid anyway. And you sure didn't attend any services when you were at camp meetings with your gram." Beercan sat back and push forth a self-satisfied face.

"I guess it don't make any difference." Ben resumed staring at the candle. He tried to ignore the heat and the mosquitoes.

Beercan waited for a few minutes before asking the next question. It was a sore subject, but Ben brought it up, so he would have to answer. "So what about you and Tahsanchat?"

"Shut up."

Beercan wouldn't let it go. He grunted in a nasty way. "She never liked you anyway. You guys were doomed. You're just a dumb, lazy Indian who dropped out, and she's gonna be somebody when she graduates."

Ben had nothing to say about that.

All the pop was gone. There were six blue and red empty cans surrounding the candle like a prayer circle.

A bead of sweat slid down Ben's forehead and perched on his nose before diving onto the front of his shirt. He wiped his forehead with his hand, but that just moved the moisture around. The rotting taste of the pop languished in his mouth. There was nothing in the house to wash it out. Beercan didn't pay the water bill, either. Without Michigan's ten-cent bottle return law, he might never have paid any bills.

Ben shifted around in his seat. Over the odor of the candle, he could smell rain coming. The crickets had gone quiet. He looked over at Beercan. He couldn't make out his friend's face. How long had they been sitting there, silent, staring at the candle?

Beercan stared at the candle and thought about his high school art teacher who told him that he had real talent, talent he should try to develop. The teacher offered to stay after school to help him with his painting. At first, Beercan thought it would be a real nice thing for teacher to help him out like that, maybe help him go to a good college or art school. Then the teacher moved real close to Beercan and put his hand—the one with the wedding band—on Beercan's leg.

"Thanks, Mr. Lincoln," Beercan said. "But I have to be home right after to school to help my mom."

Beercan rarely thought about college or art school, but when he did, he craved another beer or a pull from a bottle.

Ben's last job had been cleaning portable toilets at Cherry Festival in Traverse City. He made good money that week, draining the bowl, wiping down the narrow, white seats and the blue, plastic walls with chemical antibacterial agents, and replacing the empty TP containers with more cheap paper. He got used to the smell after the first day, though each successive day of the festival was hotter than before and the concomitant odor that much worse.

The cash Ben made that week was long gone. A month after the festival and he didn't know when he would see that much money again.

Ben lit another cigarette and stared at the red ash at the tip. He brought it up to his eye and looked at the ash very closely. The smoke and the heat began to burn his eye, so he put it down and held it between his fingers on his lap. He blinked a couple times and then took a long drag. A wretched cough shook him as the smoke filled his lungs, forcing him to drop the cigarette and bend over in pain.

Beercan stomped it out with his boot before the previous week's issue of the *TV Guide* caught on fire. He didn't have a TV anymore, but the *TV Guides* kept coming in the mail. He thought about stapling them to the wall. They would make good insulation.

"When are you gonna fix the screen door?"

Beercan shrugged.

Ben couldn't really see him in the dim light, but he knew what Beercan meant. In the house on Badder Road, nothing ever got fixed. "You know, this is one old Indian house. They should turn it into a reservation. We're out here in the middle of nowhere, just a coupla 'Nishinaabes in a rundown shack. Who would care if we made it our own reservation?"

Beercan shrugged again, still staring at the light.

Ben nodded, seeing his friend's point. "Then again, who would care if we didn't?" His eye still burned from the hot coals and smoke from his cigarette. He was so tired, and it was so humid he couldn't sleep. His eyes burned from being awake all day and all night.

Beercan said, "Auto mechanic school doesn't sound too bad, actually."

"What the hell are you talking about?"

"Both my uncles were real good mechanics. Before the cars all went computerized, they always fixed all of our cars. They tried to teach me how to change the oil, but I can't remember anymore."

"No way," Ben said. "You need to go to art school. I was at the gallery in Northport, and they sell paintings for five, six hundred dollars. And they sell black and white photos at Kejara's Bridge for seventy-five, sometimes a hundred bucks. That's where the cash is. Forget auto mechanic school."

Beercan thought about the last painting he made. He never really finished it, but it was supposed to look like the sunset over Lake Michigan, with Pyramid Point on the left and South Manitou Island on the right. All he could remember was that he got drunk one night and showed it to some college girl from Northwestern Michigan College in his bedroom at his uncle's place on Setterbo Road a few years back. He didn't remember what happened, but he never saw the painting again. In fact, he had forgotten about the whole thing, probably on purpose. He swallowed hard.

The blue morning light crept into the room slowly, long after the candle had burned out. Ben's eyes had closed hours before, and he had slumped further into his seat.

Beercan didn't sleep. He hardly ever slept anymore. He'd been thinking about Tahsanchat, about how she was down in Ann Arbor, studying economics, probably the first Indian to understand the New York Stock Exchange. Ben wouldn't know if he went down to see her. He knew Ben would sleep all day if no one roused him. Beercan collected the six cans, grasped his friend's car keys so as not to wake him and walked out the front door. He wouldn't be coming back. Not for a long while.

End of the World Resort

I am lying in bed in Ballard when she tells me to go to the airport and wait for her.

I don't understand, but I say "OK," like I know what she's talking about. So confusing. The world is about to end, and I'm not really sure I want to be at the airport when it does.

She dashes around the house, collecting small but important items for us—passports, bank statements, credit cards—and I stare at her. She stops and looks back at me. "Go. Just get over there. Wait for me. Just go now." She shoos me out the door like you shoo a cat.

"How?"

"Drive your car."

"OK," I say, trying to keep calm. Right. I have a car. I could do that.

She hugs me. I feel more love in that hug than I have ever felt from anyone or anything else.

I walk like a satisfied zombie out into the street where I see my car, dusty with rain splatters, parked under a tree. Haven't driven this car in months. I begin driving, pulling out onto the arterial heading toward Fremont, formerly the center of the universe, and the Aurora Bridge.

Nevertheless, motorists clog the roads for miles, and traffic backs up a full mile before I can guide my car over the bridge. The motorists act wild and crazy, not like Steve Martin and Dan Ackroyd, but insane with fear and desperation, like how the Indians at Wounded Knee and Sand

Creek probably felt when the shooting started. I squint at the carnage as if watching television. It doesn't seem real to me. My brain is so fuzzy. I imagine the chances of finding her at airport are not good, but I feel no tinge of regret or sadness. I have made my peace. I am glad for that after seeing the horrible expressions of bewilderment and extreme anxiety on the faces of the motorists around me.

I look around for police and see none. I remember films and stories about the end of the world, the collapse of the industrial society, and expect white men wearing short sleeve shirts and striped ties carrying shotguns will approach my slow-moving vehicle and shoot at me or others for no other reason than they don't feel like themselves anymore.

None of that happens.

Off to my left, a truck heading in the opposite direction rams into another truck, and they both careen off the side of the bridge right about where a bus went over a few years ago.

I wonder where the army guys are. There're always army guys in these movies.

I see boats down below on the canal, fighting for space to get out into Puget Sound and the ocean and Canada or wherever. Away from Seattle.

Seattle will be a big target. Many bombs will explode here. I wonder if Rainier will explode.

No one can say why the world is ending. No one really knows. Accidents just happen. Everything has to end somewhere. Somehow.

I drive and meander my way down the highway for several hours until I reach Sea-Tac.

Cars and trucks stop traffic about a mile from the terminal. Everyone seems to be getting out and walking or running.

I remain calm. I get out and walk. People carrying large suitcases and still holding onto their Porsche keys push me down, trying to get past me between a Cadillac SUV and a super-large pickup. I dust myself off and keep walking, always letting pass those behind me who run and scream and shout.

I arrive at the terminal. Everyone at the front of the ticket lines seems to be asking the few remaining people at the ticket counters for the next available flight out of Seattle.

I stand around and view the spectacle of activity around me, the airport a giant organism of wails and a low, angry roar. People rush by me carrying small children, garbage bags of clothes, holding out tickets to prove they have a reservation. Everyone wants to go to Australia or New Zealand or Canada or obscure parts of Idaho or Wyoming. No one wants to go to DC or San Francisco or Houston or Phoenix or Tokyo or Mexico City or Hawaii. I see older people giving up their seats to younger people, and young people giving up their seats to children, and men giving up their seats to women, and couples giving up their seats so they can stay together. I see people fighting. I see people giving up. I see people praying. I see danger and excitement.

I see her approach with a serious man carrying a gun.

I smile at her. She is so beautiful.

"Come with me. I've taken care of everything. We have to go now."

The people in the airport give us a wide berth because of the serious man with the big gun. She carries nothing on her and pulls me along.

I am not even sure if I love her. Love doesn't seem to matter anymore.

We walk for what seems like hours. It seems like hours because we rush, hustling down the stale corridors now filled with frantic, hopeless humanity. We swerve, left and right, left again, and through a collection of people begging for a seat, just one goddam seat, please, don't you have any generosity left in your body, for my kid, for my wife, go to hell, assholes.

On the plane. The pilot jerks the jumbo-jet through the crowded airfield, cutting off smaller planes and road vehicles that try to hijack big jets, desperate for a ride, a lift out of this place. I worry that I might die on this plane. I want to see the sky when I die. I don't tell her this. I must be strong. I look at her. She holds her face forward, not a touch of nerves anywhere. I see the other passengers gripping their partners, their seats, their armrests, expecting a bumpy ride.

She whispers one thing to me over the whine of the jet engines as we taxi.

"The missiles could launch at any time."

We might not even get off the ground. We might not have anywhere to land. We might crash because of the shockwave from an atomic blast. We might fly into an atomic fireball. We might make it.

I whisper. "Where are we going?"

I know she had connections, had a way to save us from the fate of so many others. A sudden, burning fate. Or a fate following that, the slow, torturous death from chemical poisoning or famine or murder.

"Don't worry. If we get there, we're taken care of. I've taken care of everything."

Jets take off side by side. Smaller planes take off from the taxi lanes. Once in the air, our plane swerves once, twice, three times, to avoid collisions and thunderclouds.

I sleep.

I awaken on approach to a tropical place near an ocean. I see jets swirling around us. I hear someone say they saw a missile coming. I hear another say that's bullshit; shut up, you hysterical bastard.

I grip the armrest.

She does her breathing exercises, soothing her mind and body.

I focus with my settled mind, the one I acquired in Seattle after she told me to go to the airport, the one that doesn't care anymore.

I see planes to my left out the window, fighting for position, trying to land before the explosions come and mess up everyone's instruments with that accursed electro-magnetic pulse. I can almost feel the thoughts coming from the cockpit.

Just get it down and slam the brakes.

Just get it down and slam the brakes.

Just a few more seconds.

A few more seconds.

Bump. Bump. Bump. Squeal. We roll to a halt.

She tells me to close my eyes.

BOOM.

White light.

Quiet cabin. The flight attendants ask us to remove our seatbelts and move toward the front of the plane. We will be using the emergency exits and taking the big, yellow chutes down to the tarmac.

She holds my hand. I feel that she does not love me like she used to. I don't love her like I used to. She knows that.

We accept this.

We survived.

On the tarmac, a woman wearing tacky vacation clothes welcomes us to the resort.

"I'm so glad you two made it," the woman says as though she knows us.

We fake-smile and follow the woman, away from the other passengers.

"Things aren't going well in the world," the woman says, as though chatting with old friends about unimportant subjects, conversational tidbits recommended to her from an etiquette primer.

She engages with the woman in a dispassionate talk about the damage done while I follow them to the small airport terminal and then to a resort hotel.

We don't check in. A resort employee who seems to know us already takes us all the way up to our room, a room that looks like any other hotel room. It smells nice, like fake flowers. The woman hugs us both with sincere, friendly warmth. She smells like the room.

No idea how all this came to be and I don't ask.

We are at the fringes of the world.

I know the hotel has something to do with her propensity for preparedness, as if we're cashing in on an insurance policy. Just in case. I suppose the other guests in this place bought the same insurance policy. I wonder why she chose me to be with her. I'm not special. I can tell a good joke. That's about it.

We dress in new clothes we find in the dressers and head down to the hotel restaurant for lunch.

The sun shines with an intensity I'm not used to. The gentle breeze rolls off the ocean and smells sweet. The air feels warm and comfortable.

We eat fresh fish from the ocean for lunch.

She doesn't say much during lunch. She looks content, though, and thoughtful, like she's on vacation. Relaxing.

I know we will live the rest of our days here in this place. I do not know how long that will be. No one does. Days. Months. Years. We may all die of old age in this pleasure palace, a utopia founded by the elite. We might die in a few days, attacked by marauding rebels, killer barbarians, the jealous, fighting a class war.

We don't know and never will know when this part will end.

I see neon lights everywhere. I see that the resort only takes up about four or five square blocks. I could walk it in a few minutes. The resort employees have blocked off the roads out of town, heading up the sheer, jungle cliffs above us.

We are in complete isolation.

An Asian man wearing a white coat walks up to me carrying a telephone.

"Your parents," the man says to me like a pure professional, with just a trace of an accent.

My parents. Holy. How did they find me?

"Yes," I say, questioning into the phone.

My mother. "Where are you, son?"

"I don't know where we are."

She overhears my comment and draws a quick map on her napkin.

"We?" my mother asks.

My father's voice enters my ear. "You selfish bastard. You sit there eating shellfish while we rot away from radiation from Chicago and Detroit."

I hear the phone scraping on the floor somewhere in Michigan.

My mother again. "Son, where are you?"

I look at the map she has drawn. I don't recognize any of the places on the map. Western Mediterranean? Caribbean? What? "Somewhere near the ocean," I say. "I don't know. How did you find me?"

"Your credit cards," my mom says. "Whenever you use them, we can track you. We'll find you if we have to."

"But I haven't . . ."

My mother. "I love you, boy."

"I love you, mom."

My father. "I love you, too, son. Be careful."

"Okay. I will be."

My mom again. "We'll miss you."

"Bye, mom."

Click.

The Asian man in the white coat takes the phone away.

"I won't be able to talk to them again, will I?"

She shrugs. "No. Probably not."

She tells me we're safe here for the rest of our lives. We never have to worry about a thing.

I'll live here until the end of my days. Until death.

On the edge of the world.

On the edge of death, of oblivion.

I've given my death away in exchange for resort living.

What if I get tired of fruity drinks?

What if I tire of the pool? Of the sun?

What if commit a terrible crime and don't deserve to mingle with my co-inhabitants?

What if I tire of the same fish every day? The same beer? The same water?

What if I tire of her? Of men in white coats?

What if I want to go back?

I can't leave.

Ever.

What if I tire of the resort?

What then?

She smiles at me and offers me an orange-flavored drink. I tell her that I've decided to eat meat once again. She says, "I asked for the veggie menu for you, so that's what we're getting. I thought you didn't like meat."

"Oh, I guess I don't," I say.

It'll do.

An Iranian in de Gaulle

The Iranian shifted his bottom a little to the left. He was sore, sitting there all day, and knew it was time to walk around, get some exercise. Instead, he scratched his long, dirty beard and concentrated on reading an intriguing African's strange and exciting interpretation of *The Bacchae*. He would get up and move around later, after he finished the book. He would need to move around later anyway. One should always dangle at least a little bit. It helps to digest the book.

The Iranian had plenty of time to think.

It was Tuesday.

The American college girl spoke French to the Iranian. She figured he was Moroccan or something, and a Moroccan in de Gaulle airport most definitely understood French. The Iranian, who definitely understood French and delighted in speaking the language, was definitely not Moroccan.

They conversed in French until her plane began boarding. The Iranian was not sad by her departure.

It was Sunday.

The Iranian read a discarded copy of the *New York Times*. He had been reading discarded copies of the *New York Times* for three thousand eight hundred seventy-two days consecutively. People always seemed to discard the *New York Times* more so than other papers, but the Iranian did not stop to question his bounty. He became keenly aware of the so-called liberal bias of the American media and how Americans truly hated Iran and, generally, most other countries.

It had been a long week since his last good cleaning. The Iranian was lazy and knew it, relished it.

It was Thursday.

The Iranian intently studied a German beer advertisement. He never consumed alcoholic beverages and never had any intent to ever do so. Yet, as he studied the page in the magazine loaded with words he did not understand, he vaguely felt the urge to drink a frosty mug of German lager. He had been offered booze before but had always politely declined. What was the poetic value of beer advertisements? The Iranian turned to his handy Gideon Bible for answers.

It was Sunday again.

"Where are you going, my fellow traveler?" the nuclear physicist from Bonn asked the Iranian in English, their common language. The Iranian had met this German physicist before, but he could not remember when. It must have been a few years, at least. The Iranian did remember that this German was a charming fellow, well worth conversing with. The Iranian noticed the German's English had improved since their last meeting.

"I see your English has improved."

The German was somewhat startled, but then realized he had indeed met the Iranian before. "We've met before, have we not?"

The Iranian smiled a gentle affirmative. "Yes. I remember you as a German physicist. A German physicist that travels extensively."

The German laughed out loud and habitually picked at his beard in a way that reminded the Iranian of Freud. "We probably met in an airport, didn't we?"

The Iranian nodded.

It was Monday.

The beautiful flight attendant from Nice sat down next to the Iranian like she always did. She stopped asking dumb personal questions long ago, when they began their bond. She said little more than hello and goodbye during the visit but left the Iranian with a few books on Tibetan mysticism and ancient Aztec economics. He really had wanted to hear a song by her favorite band, the Butthole Surfers, but hid his disappointment. After she left wearily to go to her home and rest, he turned eagerly to his new books. The Iranian knew he would have to study hard. These books were in Spanish Catalan.

It was Friday.

"You fell asleep again, my dear friend," the Belgian woman said to the Iranian in gutter French-Dutch. "My newspaper," the Iranian whispered, still groggy from his narcoleptic fit. He shook his head to clear cobwebs.

"Gone, I'm afraid," the Belgian informed him. Her mind was already drifting back to her work. The Iranian hoped he would be able to find another copy of *Le Monde* before the end of the day. They were hard to come by.

It was Wednesday.

The Iranian munched on the jam-covered baguette, dripping red raspberry juice on the battered pages of Thomas Lynch's collection of mortuary comedy. The Iranian keenly wanted to see the Huron River now. He realized it was likely the first time in a decade he had wished fervently to see any particular landscape at all. He was content where he was. And he knew Dulles Airport was as close as he would ever get to the Huron River.

The Belgian woman approached with a cappuccino and a pensive air. The Iranian gulped down that last of his airport meal and quietly belched with pleasure.

It was Wednesday again.

The Iranian conversed with a Thai psychologist in French, their common language. The Thai female was deeply impressed with the Iranian's knowledge of Buddhist psychological theory. The Iranian was equally impressed with the Thai female's knowledge of Japanese military history. They spoke to each other for hours, engrossed in each other's diverse knowledge. The Thai psychologist missed her plane to Athens and barely noticed. They played cards while they talked, almost as a sidebar to the real spectacle above the seat. The Iranian revealed his distress at his past treatment at the hands of his religious leader, and the Thai female openly wept in sympathy.

Of course, the Iranian eventually fell asleep. When he awoke, the flight attendant from Nice was sitting with him, gently holding his hand and making sure no one took the book she had brought for him, her good friend. The Iranian was pleased.

It was Bastille Day.

The Iranian listened patiently to the Italian boy as he cried his eyes out. The Iranian did not understand Italian very well at all, but he guessed accurately what this boy's problem was. The Italian boy was very young and eventually cried himself to sleep. The Iranian softly moved the boy to a comfortable place and took up Dostoyevsky's first, intent on relearning Russian.

The airport police took the Italian boy away an hour later and nodded a terse acknowledgment to the Iranian.

It was Tuesday again.

Le Monde sent a beat reporter to make sure the Iranian was still at the airport. The Iranian had previously promised three other reporters from the papers that he would notify them if he ever had a notion to leave. He nevertheless enjoyed a visitation from a reporter as he found interviews an enlightening process. The reporter's name was Rita.

Nevertheless, the Iranian was unable to answer a single question.

It was Tuesday again.

The Brazilian woman drinking red wine blew the Iranian away. She had a beautiful and innocent smile, broad and toothy. Downright shameless. The Iranian knew she was much too young for him and a Catholic to boot. She was very shy at first, but never moved away.

"Why Paris?" the Iranian asked in English, wishing he were younger, more casual around women, and capable of going where she was going.

"To learn French. And to study art." The Brazilian had curly black hair and was one of those troubling people that made drinking look cool.

"Ah. I have been studying art since I landed here. At one time, I had books on Caravaggio, Munch, Zuni Fetishes, and a tour guide from the Uffuzi. I've had other books, but they were stolen before I could read them."

The Brazilian eyed the Iranian's current book. "What are you reading now?"

"A book about American Indians. It's very sad. This may be the angriest book I have ever read. Funny, too."

The Brazilian examined the cover. As she thought, she spoke. "I knew an American once. Long ago. A few years anyway. Met him in Venezia."

"Ah, Venice. It is as beautiful as they say?"

"Yes."

"How is your French?" the Iranian asked in French.

"Not very good," the Brazilian answered, also in French. In English, she added, "I have been to France only once before. I was here to see the World Cup, to see Ronaldo and Brazil."

The Iranian remembered the World Cup well. 1998. France was crazy. Paris was crazy.

It was Friday.

A man from the northeastern part of Canada said he would replenish the Iranian's travel bag in exchange for a good story. The Iranian told the story that starts with the woman with the four-year-old named Ernest. She was a single mother, her husband dying at the childbirth of their son, in nineteenth-century Amsterdam. She had a terrible time of it, even though the husband had left a rapacious fortune. Her family was elsewhere and no support at all. His family subtly blamed her for the death and made Amsterdam a hostile habitat. Society shunned them so the tiny outcast family found social refuge with carnival folk.

Ernest's mother had a large estate, and she would offer space on the vast acreage to travelers from everywhere and anywhere. No one liked drifters in those days, unlike now. No one liked single moms, either, especially ones with spoiled, obnoxious children. It was a perfect match.

But to say Ernest was spoiled and obnoxious was unfair. He was much, much worse than that. From the time he began walking and talking, Ernest was surrounded by men and women of the world. They taught him gutter dialects of Dutch, French, Flemish, pig Latin. They taught him card tricks, dice tricks, how to throw his voice. How to wear dirty hats at odd but charming angles. How to remove women's undergarments quickly and with only a modicum of fuss. They taught him to lie, to juggle, to pick pockets. They taught Ernest these things not because traveling people survived on illicit activity, but because someone like that little boy will eventually need to know those things.

And Ernest was a very quick learner. He learned how to cry and evoke sympathy from strangers. He also learned short snippets of French love poetry and the Koran to delight and befuddle his victims. The Iranian noted to the Canadian that Ernest was colder and more skilled than even the little girl vampire in the Anne Rice novel.

By the time Ernest was four, he could take everything out of his mother's pockets without her ever knowing. He was a young grifter and could smell a mark a mile away. His mother was concerned that the boy was growing up with a calloused, conscience-free heart but was jaded enough on Amsterdam residents so that she couldn't wait to unleash an older, mature Ernest on that foul city.

It came to pass that the snotty side of Ernest's family began to question openly the education of Ernest by all them scary travelers. They started inviting Ernest's mother, who was still very young and gullible, to social gatherings in hopes that some mature gentleman would swoop in, grab her, and teach her right. It was obvious to everyone involved with Ernest's mother that the boy required a statelier hand to further his upbringing. For example, his accent was just wrong. And his French was downright frightful.

The Canadian listener noted to the Iranian that he spoke French rather well and that French was beautifully spoken by Canadian children. The Iranian, annoyed that the Canadian would be so rude as to interrupt the story, made a snide comment about French Canadians and also about Celine Dion and, before long, the Canadian walked away, suddenly grumpy.

The Iranian only told stories about men and boys named Ernest.

It was Friday.

A resident of Amsterdam reading a bullshit commentary on *The Waste Land* sat next to the Iranian. She looked bored and confused by her text and seemed to look bored and confused as a pretext for casual conversation. The Iranian saw it coming two hundred miles away. He started humming "You Can't Hurry Love" and farted loudly, lifting the leg and rump nearest the Amsterdam resident, as he reached for his economics treatise. The Amsterdam resident looked surprised for a second and then laughed heartily out loud. She laughed louder and harder. It was the Iranian's turn to look surprised for a second. He then smiled. The Amsterdam resident kept laughing and even gripped her stitching side. Airport passersby stopped to look at the red-headed Amsterdam resident. Some, mostly Americans, even gawked. The Iranian smiled even more broadly.

When she finally stopped laughing, the Amsterdam resident had many interesting things to say to the Iranian. She told him about the boy from Nebraska, who was on her last flight whose arm smelled like fish. She said she waited three hours on the flight from Dulles for the boy to fall asleep, so she could sniff his arm to be absolutely certain. She said the book she was reading was terribly boring and contrite, but she felt obligated to read the goddam thing because a long, lost uncle had written it in 1967. She said she mostly read sex manuals. They were the most interesting and useful books, and they almost always had illustrations. She said she had never been a student, having dropped out of school in Detroit, as soon as she learned how to read. Tenth grade. She told wonderful and grisly stories of escape from truant officers prowling Tiger Stadium in second grade and DEA officers walking on the Detroit River wharfs in seventh grade. She said heroin was much better than sex, and it better be, because it made the user impotent. She said she had been an actress once she dropped out of high school for good and had done a few Dayton-Hudson's commercial spots.

The Iranian was envious in a fundamental way of the Amsterdam resident's tales and told her ridiculous lies to compensate. The girl could see the Iranian liked her, so she told him another story. Her plane was delayed several hours. She might even have to stay in an airport hotel for the night. She had been told by her good friend Ruben in DC that the baggies in her stomach would pop out the next shit she took. She wanted to know if the Iranian would snort a little smack with her after she went to the bathroom and took a dump. Just a little, she warned, because the H was uncut. And soon because she really needed to shit now. She said she hated having to hold it anymore.

The Iranian said he would think about it.

It was Tuesday again.

When the Iranian awoke late in the afternoon, the book on airline crashes the beautiful flight attendant from Nice had given him was, of course, gone. He searched diligently and felt sad the book was gone. The Iranian enlisted the aid of two Australian teenagers carrying far too much crap. They found nothing. The Iranian offered them some pure, uncut heroin, but they politely declined. Instead, they told boring and disgusting stories about Venezia and American Indians.

It was Wednesday.

The Moroccan gentleman, wearing a fez perfectly, looked annoyed when the Iranian asked for the time in French.

"I've seen you here before," the Moroccan said. "The man who cannot leave de Gaulle."

The Iranian chuckled in spite of the state he was in. "Yes, it's true. I cannot leave. A Catholic would say I am in limbo."

"It's been a long time. Ten years?"

"Yes. Ten years since Morocco denied my application."

The Moroccan spoke about his children, the disinterested and decidedly unmotivated lawyer and the corrupt import businessman, after the Iranian politely asked.

The Moroccan looked like a man who had lived a long, worldly life, but the Iranian would not offer him any heroin.

It was Monday.

A Vietnamese woman had left a large pile of women's magazines lying about. The Iranian inspected them thoroughly, enjoying the French language, French perfume, French food, and Italian lingerie. The Parisian flight attendant, who spoke a little Arabic, smiled in mischief when she saw the Iranian staring with a fearsome hunger at the glossy pages.

"What do you think you are doing?" the Parisian asked in Arabic.

Embarrassed, the Iranian smiled meekly and uttered, "I am living vicariously."

It was Wednesday.

Lola searched the airport for the Iranian and was about to give up when she saw him lying under a row of seats, mouth agape and slightly snoring. She felt a terrific sense of relief that the Iranian was still in the airport. She was worried that the work she had done for him was all for nothing.

And, of course, Lola had some other problems that could only be resolved by the wise counsel of a stranded Iranian political refugee who had lost his papers. She took a deep breath and sat down near the Iranian to await his awakening.

Patience.

Lola met the Iranian nearly ten years earlier, when she was only twenty years old. She had traveled the globe since then, visiting such places as Cambodia, Greece, Nepal, New Mexico. He was a curiosity then, able to purchase sex and liquor but unable to consume either. Lola fell in love with the Iranian then and helped him search the airport for his papers. She had seen the Iranian thrice since, the last time three years previous when she vowed not to return until she had a damn good reason—amnesty papers or a cure for narcolepsy or a large, incomprehensible concern in her life.

Lola waited for hours, reading a book written by her best friend that was immature, condescending, confusing, and generally sucked. How would she tell him? She eventually stopped reading and considered which language she would converse with when the Iranian woke. Her Arabic had improved dramatically, and her French was always good. She had brought a few presents for the Iranian that he could enjoy immediately. She knew nothing lasted long with him, except his empty, worn-out travel bag.

"Lola, is it you?" the Iranian muttered in Arabic fondly, startling her.

Lola accepted the Arabic language challenge like a teenage chess master who is asked to play a septuagenarian grandmaster. "I am well, my friend. And you? Still going through whores like a poet goes through whiskey?"

The Iranian laughed. "Your Arabic is better, but I see such a beautiful language plainly could not cure your foul mouth."

Lola smiled broadly and embraced her part-time mentor, not sure what the Iranian had just said but unwilling to show it. "I see your harem of flight attendant women has deserted you, my insect-ridden, dope-addled friend."

"It is true they do not treat me so well anymore."

"Yes, impotence is a sad thing, but a virile man should be able to overcome its terrible ravages."

"Alas, the amphetamines have failed me."

"I see, judging from seeing you asleep in a puddle of your own filth underneath a row of airport seating, that the vicious addiction to female genitals has left you exhausted and dirty."

"True, but I live for it, hot and wet."

"I see why lowly, worthless scum like you was booted from the simple goodness of Iran."

"It's very good to see you again."

“Sick as it is, I was worried you would be gone.”

“I wait for you, my friend.”

Lola dug through her pack, excited by her news. She pulled out some stamped papers. “Belgium has granted you asylum.”

The Iranian could not speak. Instead, he carefully inspected the papers, knowing that he would eventually lose them. If he were to leave, he better do it soon.

If.

“I also have a problem,” Lola said sadly. “But you knew already, didn’t you?”

“What problem?”

The international terminal was very busy at that moment, with hordes of steaming, angry passengers milling around like bees that smell kerosene and realize the whole shithouse is in trouble. Lola didn’t want to talk over the wretched din, so she waited. The Iranian, who had been waiting for over a decade, sat quietly next to her.

A Filipino boy with an Action Man doll ran through the lobby, putting everyone in hazardous straits as they avoided his clumsy advance. Lola laughed suddenly and decided her shit wasn’t so bad after all. She watched the boy bounce around, crashing into the airport occupants like waves on grumpy rocks. Unstoppable. Uncaring. Laughing at the idiocy around him.

The Iranian casually opened a book on Ojibwe mysticism while the Filipino boy fucked about. He was thinking that, even though he had more time to kill than anyone else he planned to use it efficiently. He read on, even after the Filipino boy settled down—or was settled down by his embarrassed guardians—and waited for Lola’s soliloquy. He read on and on and almost came to the conclusion that American Indians were absolute lunatics, but reserved judgment, ultimately, until he could actually meet an Ojibwe person. Eventually, as he always did, the Iranian slept.

When the Iranian woke, it was Thursday, and Lola was gone.

The Italian male and his Irish girlfriend looked completely wired to the Iranian when they sat down in the front row of seats near the Air France gate with the big brown coffee stain on the wall. They were giggling wildly, but the Iranian could tell they were exceptionally annoyed with each other. She had the filthy, dirty blonde hair and laughed like a teenager trying to make it with a handsome, tough, unreachable youth with a bad mustache. He was older and bald and somehow stuck between emotional immaturity and having too much cynical life experience for his own good. They looked poor, but the Iranian wasn't fooled. People like that do not often show up in de Gaulle with international tickets.

The Iranian reminded himself that he had hidden away three baggies of pure, uncut heroin and also that he could use some money. People as strung out and desperate for some experimental stimulation as the two he viewed before him would no doubt be intrigued by an offer from a lapsed Iranian for some very cheap and very white powder. The Iranian struggled with his conscience for a time. What would become of these two young lovers? He wanted to imagine them paying him well and having a dangerous but harmless heroin joyride, with no long-term side effects. Lots of people simply just tried it once for the sake of saying to potential love scores that they tried it, the Iranian rationalized. Of course, many first-time uses ended up with gaping sores in the crooks of their arms and a terrible willingness to perform unspeakable sex acts in exchange for the opportunity to let a fellow junky inject a dirty, globular hit into their eyeball or stomach. But that kind of hideous failure was rare—it *had* to be. More likely, the couple would try it together the first time and then just sell or give away the rest to some reasonable friends. Or maybe, since the Iranian was selling the smack at such a reasonable price, they would simply consider the purchase an investment, taking the baggies back to Cork or Napoli to have an expert cut the white and resell it at a gigantic profit to Irish or Italian junkies. At least, this couple would come out of it OK, and the Iranian would have no privity of disaster.

The Iranian could live with that outcome.

The couple kissed and fondled each other foolishly while the Iranian stood up and walked—no, strode—to the secret hiding place to pick up his stash. As the Iranian walked—no, strode—past the couple, two events took place. Lola waved hello as she exited the little girls' room, and heavily-armed French police-soldiers triumphantly displayed the crazy-pure and uncut heroin to their supervisor, a humorless employee of the state who dreamed of writing a comedic autobiography.

The bald Italian diverted his attention from the Irish woman long enough to gaze in wide-eyed wonder at the freshly-discovered baggies of china white. Actual white heroin. Amazing. A sight to behold and the Italian appreciated the sight.

"How are you, my friend," Lola asked in Arabic, shedding the nasty insults from the day before. She wiped her still-wet hands on her jeans.

"It is an odd day," the Iranian responded in English with genuine sadness and remorse. "An odd day."

The Irish woman reminded the Italian male that he was to be giving his full attention to her. Lola looked past the Iranian to get a glimpse of them for a few seconds before taking the Italian's hand and leading him to a safer, quieter place.

"My friend," Lola stated, "I have been thinking about the story about the boy from Amsterdam. I have been thinking about that boy for three years. What the *fuck* does that story mean?"

The Iranian chuckled. "You must understand that I was raised an Arab. An Arab of Islam. Islam, like any form of religion or science, is very inconsistent with Western, industrialized democracies. There is no better setting for a fable on the folly of society than Western, industrialized democracies. And, in my humble and disgraced opinion, what Islam needs is a touch of Zen Buddhism to make it more modern and flexible. And the thing about Zen is . . . shit happens. The story is the epitome of practical application of my theory of the indictment of Western, industrialized democracies through and by a threat of Zen Buddhism."

"You're full of shit."

It was Friday.

The Iranian witnessed another tense screaming match between two halves of a married couple. He had witnessed hundreds, and each argument-voiced-as-cutting-blade hurt him as much as the participants. Each argument witnessed was a foul temptation to intervene—toss a welcome voice of reason into a bad situation, create a remedy where before there was a terrible, evil war. In the Iranian's first year at de Gaulle hundreds of years ago, he watched the arguments between people in

French, Norwegian, Egyptian, Arabic, Spanish, English, Portuguese, Japanese, Indian, and a host of other languages he could not understand. Each time he cursed himself for his cowardice. Of course, he reasoned, a fresh, rational point of view would diffuse horribly wretched scenes. They were simply unnecessary. By the Iranian's second year, he had worked up the courage to intervene a few times.

Stupid.

This day, the Iranian listened to the Americans scream at each other for a few minutes before he stood. It is better to not try talking sense to arm-flailing lunatics. He knew better now—through difficult experience. He walked away to a part of the terminal where he would not have to hear them or anyone.

It was Sunday.

The American woman who sat next to the Iranian was plainly and clearly and simply foul with pathetic hopelessness. It had been a few sleepy, miserable days since the Iranian felt like speaking to anyone, but he asked about this woman's trip, the standard conversation-starting rigmarole.

"I'm running away. My life has turned into a bad horror film, and I must get away. I know that sounds . . ."

The American woman trailed off and shook her head in a pathetic manner, like a 1960s French mime. Unlike many mimes, the American followed the gesture with a bad horror film premise.

"Six months ago, I was a victim of a hit-and-run. I suffered head injuries and spent six months in the hospital. I also was in a coma for a few days. When I awoke, I was surrounded by my loved ones, but something seemed off, not quite right. I returned their offers of support and affection, but . . . well . . ."

"Where are you from? Was the driver ever prosecuted?"

The American woman looked suspiciously at the Iranian. "I'm not gonna tell the likes of you where I'm from. None of your goddam business."

The Iranian shrugged politely, trying not to aggravate the paranoid American.

"And no, the bastard fucker was never found, but I think I know who he is."

"Well? Who?"

"I'll get to that. You hafta hear the whole story first, or it won't make any sense."

The Iranian forcibly suppressed a shudder after hearing the American's nasal rendition of the English language that suggested some awful midwestern US background, probably rural Wisconsin. He idly wondered if cheese consumption contributed enough crap to the brain to have a tendency to create paranoid episodes or overall paranoia. Something he had read a few years ago made him think that.

"I finally figured out what was different—my family and my friends. *They* were different."

The American's eyes bulged. The Iranian could not stop himself from squirming.

"You see?!? It was *so* evil! Some organization or something totally replaced everyone I knew and loved and trusted with . . . someone else. They looked like my people, but there was always something off about them. Something like hair color or mannerisms. They had worked hard to trick me, like they studied my family for some time to get it exactly right, but no one—I mean no one—can perfectly imitate someone else."

The Iranian nodded. It was true, and he figured he had better acknowledge what may have been the one bit of truth seeping from this American's collagen-enhanced lips.

"So you see why I had to run."

"I do."

It was Tuesday.

The Iranian had a difficult time understanding the Scotsman describe his putrid hate of Man United but was intrigued by the Scot's love of football. Love is still love, an imperfect emotion by imperfect beings, but as close as they would ever get, likely. The Iranian wrote poems in his head about love. Love of men and women. Love of children. Animals and trees. Baseball. But not spaghetti string tops. God hates those, too.

The Scot offered to buy lunch for them both, and the Iranian offered the story about Ernest. The Iranian reached the part where Ernest was about to be kidnapped by Amsterdam's high society when he paused, recalling in his mind the annoying Canadian.

As the Iranian paused, the Scot heard his named called out over the PA and dashed away, mumbling apologies. The Iranian smiled, happy with the trade of lunch for an incomplete story. He would keep the ending of the story for later, about how Ernest had been kidnapped by a few hired goons and driven to society.

Engulfed in Amsterdam society, Ernest became a young rebel. One evening while he was dressing for a dinner party, he drank four shots of pure Russian vodka and got totally fucked up. The boy had a fondness for peaches that he suddenly could not control. He had to have one, that instant, before the vodka robbed his ten-year-old tongue of taste buds. The party was stilted and stunted inside, party crashers waited patiently outside, but Ernest never appeared stage left.

They found him the next day, his face bloated and purple. Heimlich was alive then, but living and working in Germany or some other place.

It was Friday.

Lola returned. The Iranian watched her approach as she descended an escalator. She smiled at him. She handed his asylum papers to him and greeted him in Arabic. He sat down and read his papers. They were written in French. He had not seen any papers like these with his name on them for three thousand nine hundred eighty-seven days.

When the airline called their flight several minutes later, Lola and the Iranian boarded without incident. The instant that the Iranian crossed the threshold into the jet, he realized he hadn't been outside, breathing open air, for a very, very long time. He settled down next to an Irish woman who had the aisle seat and Lola, who had the window.

As soon the Iranian heard the electronic bleep that announced to the flight attendants that the plane had reached a height of 10,000 feet, Lola dropped off into her dreams. The Iranian let her use his soft shoulder for a pillow and eagerly grasped his copy of a memoir about Indian child removals written by an Odawa woman named Wenona. He could never sleep on planes.

Ten-Year Visit

Mom's house on Christmas Day. Seems like fifty relatives over. I remember some of the older ones, but anyone under ten wouldn't have been born when I left. My eyes are blurry from fatigue, the twenty-four-hour trip home. I don't really know any of the people in the room. They're all ten years older than they were when I knew them. They've changed. I find it best to sit and not attract attention. Aunt Maggie is the nosiest. She wants to know where I've been since 1993. She still talks too loud. I don't recognize her at first because she has gained one hundred pounds. Her husband, my mother's brother, Uncle Charles, tells her to leave me alone. It is the kindest act of my holiday.

Phone rings in the morning. A man, who was my friend nearly twenty years ago, says he wants to have coffee at Bell's, the diner, like the old days. They called him Elder, the oldest son. We don't recognize each other anymore. He could be an imposter. The first thing he tells me is that all of our old friends from Wayland High School are gone. He says it's just him and me now. I want a glass of wine and hashish. I tell him that, in Wayland, it's still just him. I leave tomorrow. He says we should go out tonight then. He's thirty-five and balding. He's overweight, more so than he was in high school after he quit the track team to focus on his writing. He works at the gas station, changing oil and flushing out radiators. I say it would be okay if he calls me later, and I leave the diner.

Kathy Spellings kissed me at Bell's when I was sixteen. She had a round belly and strong wrists. She was a brown Indian like me, a part of an Anishinaabe tribe that was administratively terminated, whatever that means. She had long, black hair she tied into a ponytail when she played tennis. Like me, she ate too much cheese pizza and strawberry ice cream to be thin, but, unlike me, she was quick as a cat. Elder was her first boyfriend. I tried to forgive him then, but I gave up.

Kathy was my first girlfriend. In tenth grade, if I could have, I would have killed Elder. Elder is a mechanic now and was then, too, but back then he was also a poet. That's what he told everyone. He talked about the pain in his life. His mother's death. His father's failing garage. His alcoholic younger brother. He only wrote down one poem that I know of. And I know he didn't write it. He copied it out of an old edition of *Norton's Anthology*, a book I bought him at a yard sale for a quarter. It was something by the guy who wrote "Death Be Not Proud."

In high school, Elder was a whore. With that one poem, a big cheesy smile, and his sad family stories, he seduced girls all over west Michigan. Now that I think about it, I still hate Elder. Now Elder has grease stuck in his fingertips and under his nails. Permanent grease.

Since I've been home, I bet I've spoken less than one hundred words. In high school, I would sometimes go days without speaking. Everyone I knew was used to it, so they didn't bother me about it. When I go home to Amsterdam to my wife Carol, I will speak thousands of words a day. I will speak English, a little Dutch, a little Italian, and my wife's language, Brazilian Portuguese. In Europe, I talk all the time. Sometimes, my friends ask me to be quiet.

Tonight I will visit my sister, Elizabeth, and her family. Elizabeth was the last family member I spoke to before leaving ten years ago. She dropped me off at the airport in Chicago at the international terminal. Now she has a husband and triplets.

I watch movies with my mom all afternoon. She doesn't move around much anymore. She likes spy movies. I don't understand why. She tries to talk me into staying longer. She needs help around the house and with the yard. She says she's lonely since my father died in a plane crash last year. He wasn't really my dad. He was my step-dad. I never met him in person, but I talked to him on the phone once.

Elder calls again and tells me he'll be at Jolly Bar around nine. I say that's fine and hang up. He expects to see me there.

We have dinner at Elizabeth's house. Her husband is a nice man, but he's too confident in the stability of his life. He doesn't acknowledge that his job or family could collapse at any moment. I sometimes tell people that civilization is an anomaly and impermanent. Indians know these things. At dinner, I talk little. Elizabeth's husband is named Tom, and he has a bad goatee. He wears polo shirts and slacks. He looks like a lawyer, one who takes a laptop and a fax machine on vacation. My nieces are beautiful. They are named after my grandmother and her two sisters. I would have named them after their grandfathers to confuse people.

Elizabeth and Tom cook a vegetarian meal. I keep forgetting to tell my family that I started eating meat again a few years ago. I missed the taste, so I began to eat it again. We eat vegetarian lentil soup, vegetarian pasta, and vegan ice cream. My sister tells me she wants me to stay home and bring wasshername over here. She misses me and loves me, so I forgive her for being so selfish and insulting to my wife. Tom says nothing. I can't tell if he disagrees with Elizabeth or if he says nothing because he isn't a blood relative.

After dinner, we have Christmas. Elizabeth gives me a book signed by her friend, who attended Harvard with her. It's a screenplay with a picture of famous actors on the cover. I tell Elizabeth that I will read it on the plane tomorrow. I've already seen the film. She starts to cry. I feel bad and ask her permission to take a short walk.

Tom and my sister live near the state police station on Forrest. They live across the street from our childhood home at 524 Forrest. I go and look at our old house. It's small and ugly compared to other houses on the street. I walk south up the street toward downtown Wayland. We lived on this street for nine years. Here, I broke Steve Polson's nose. Here, I scraped most of the skin off my knee when I jumped off my bike. Here, I turned left on my way to school at Steeby Elementary. Here, through an open window, I watched a drunk lady undress and crumple into her bed. Here, I saw Denver, Markie Alexander's dog, crushed to death by a garbage truck.

Before long, I'm standing in front of Jolly Bar. I check my watch. It's only seven thirty. I look inside to see if I recognize anyone from my childhood. I see Elder. He's early. I go inside. Elders claps me on the back and orders me a drink. I prefer Grey Goose vodka in my martinis, but all they have is Stoli. The bartender serves my drink in a plastic cup, the kind we used at house parties on Greenwood in Ann Arbor.

Elder is already drunk. He talks to me about Kathy and the others he slept with when we were teenagers. It's a weekday, and only the regular drunks are there. They're much older than we are. Everyone in the bar knows Elder.

I want to hurt Elder somehow, so I challenge him to a game of pool. I'm an exceptional pool player. I defeat Elder quickly. He doesn't even sink one ball. We play again and again until Elder tires of losing every game. I can tell he's angry with me, that I won't let him even compete with me. He stops talking about teenaged women he knew and starts talking about his job—from good memories to bad reality.

The last time I was in a fight was in Tucson, Arizona. I was there to interview for a job as a law clerk for a federal judge. The fight was over a game of pool at a bar on Congress Street. I broke a chair over my adversary's head. I then broke a cue stick over his prostrate body. I would've stabbed him dead with the broken cue stick, but several large men pulled me away. I didn't get the clerkship.

I've seen many amazing things since that day. A bus explosion in Bogotá. Bloody corpses lined up for identification in South Africa. Burned corpses of smoke jumpers in Guatemala. The execution by hanging of a brutal military leader in Pakistan. I've been in hundreds, maybe thousands, of bars and dance clubs. I've witnessed dozens of fistfights and a couple of knife fights. All that and I haven't fought for over ten years.

Tonight, I will fight Elder. I will fight him until he's dead.

We leave the bar together out the back door around ten. Elder is so drunk that he can barely stand. It'll be easy for me to fight and defeat him. He directs me around the corner to his father's garage on Main Street. The street is empty. I look around for something with which to beat Elder. A blunt instrument, as they say in the movies. I see nothing until we reach the garage. Elder has trouble with the keys because his hands are unsteady, but I'm smart enough to let him open the door on his own. Inside, we walk through the garage to the back stairs. I see a pair of greasy work gloves. I also see a large wrench, almost as large as an axe.

Upstairs, Elder talks incessantly. His speech is slurred, and he staggers almost comically around the studio apartment. I calmly put on the gloves and take up the wrench, wiping it down to obscure any of my fingerprints. Elder ignores me. I turn and look at myself in his mirror over the dresser near his bed. I look strong and dangerous. I turn to face Elder, to beat him to death. It won't take long.

But I don't beat Elder to death or even raise one hand against him. In fact, I drop the large wrench onto Elder's unkempt bed and raise my gloved hands. Elder is very, very drunk. His eyes are almost closed. He can barely keep his head up off his own chest. He's sitting on his sole kitchen chair pointing a shotgun at me. The shotgun wavers a bit, but the aim is good enough to change my life forever if Elder fires it.

I ask Elder what he's doing, trying to emulate HAL 9000's calming voice. Elder's voice is so fuzzy I can't understand. I ask again. He says he wants my wallet.

I say OK, but I don't move.

Elder tells me that his life is a sack of shit, that he is poor, and he is lonely. He tells me he deserves more and that I deserve less. He says something about Kathy but can't understand him anymore. He slowly slumps forward and drops his gun. He slides to the floor next to his bed.

While I hope Elder dies of blood poisoning or asphyxiates on his own vomit, I do nothing to injure him. I replace the gloves and the wrench on my way out.

As my plane accelerates down the runway at the Gerald R. Ford (formerly Kent County) airport in the morning, I think that beating Elder to death would've been the perfect crime. By the time anyone found his pathetic corpse, I'd be in Amsterdam. I have no record, and there'd be no way for the local police to trace me. The drunks in the bar didn't know me. I would've gotten away scot-free.

Before I said goodbye this morning, I gave my mom ten thousand dollars. I told her that she could use the money for anything she wanted. I suggested that there was enough for her and Elizabeth's entire family to visit me in Amsterdam. Carol and I have a large house, for Amsterdam. I told my mother that in Amsterdam I am a different person. I'll tell her anything she wants to know. I'll entertain her and tell jokes. I'll laugh and have fun. I'll be normal.

The Village by the Sea

We watched them coming. With the cold, brisk air carrying well, my grandmother could smell their boat even over the sea surf. She said that sweat, blood, grog, and anger had soaked into the wood holding the boat together. My brother and I loved to listen to Gram, but we never believed her sense of smell could be that sharp. She said she could smell us approach from some distance away and could tell which one of us it was. She said she could smell animals in heat and when they were ready to be taken.

We loved our gram, and she led the village well. She made bread like nobody's business. My bread came out tough like bark, and we had to soak it in the soup to make it edible. Gram would sit at dinner and tell us about the tricksters and the three ancient peoples of the north—the Anishinaabeg, the Plains people, and the Chmookmanaag—and how the war-like Chmookmanaag had been driven out of the continent long before any of us had been born. Gram taught us to fish and cure venison hide. Even though our friends said it was girl stuff, she also taught us how to make baskets from porcupine quills.

From behind some rocks, we watched the boats head toward shore. They were long and narrow, with many oars protruding from the sides. We heard deep growls from inside the thing, keeping a sort of savage time with the thrusts of the oars. The long-toothed dragon wood carving heading the first boat looked almost comical. My cousin drew vicious-looking mystical beasts similar to the visitors' fearful announcement. The welcoming party, consisting of four of our most charismatic and careful men and women, immediately recognized the visitors' intentions upon sight of the dragon's long, wooden teeth.

"Chmookman," my brother said.

"Gram got us again," I said. "How does she always know?"

Gram's sense of smell derived from her inability to see. After she lost her sight at age six to the illness that periodically attacked our people, she began to focus on her sense of smell. She started to believe that she could sense odors from far away. Gram's father explained that, when one of us loses one ability, other abilities improve to compensate. He died when he accidentally stumbled onto a hibernating bear's den in spring, looking for drummer's root. Gram said she had decided not to go with him that day because she wanted to stay home and visit. She would have been able to smell the bear. She would have been able to save her father.

The five boats entered the harbor, rotting and sea-worn. Another invasion fleet, we all knew. They came to conquer, to take, to possess, to destroy, to control. We knew from their appearance and smell they'd be unreasonable and uncooperative. We could already see the swords and clubs and spikes and knives and bloodlust and greed from way back behind the rocks.

The welcoming party from the migizi doodem faded back into the woods, leaving a few of the old houses near the shore untended to see what the visitors would do. They left the houses full of bread and vegetables and meat and mead and stayed out of sight, watching from the safety of the newer homes on the hill. As we all predicted, the sailors looted and pillaged and burned, going so far as to destroy much of the offerings.

The watchers reported that the visitors ate and drank everything they got their hands on until they vomited the excess on the walls, the floors, and each other. What waste. They were pale-skinned and sickly, their hair was white, salt-bleached and filthy, and their clothing consisted of tattered rags. They looked terrible, health-wise—bad teeth, runny noses, jaundiced. They also looked battle-tested. The watchers speculated that the visitors could have originated with the Chmookmanaag, the legendary northern band that had been driven out centuries ago when they got to be too much for the rest of us. They seemed to have forgotten they had ever lived here but still had the old warlike tendencies and unintelligible speech. They used the metallurgical knowledge the old people had given them as a gift to make bigger and better weapons.

We learned their languages almost immediately. You could tell their meaning not from the spoken word but from the glint in their eyes. The words and the body language could not hide the message in the squinting, colorful eyes. We watched them carefully. These visitors had ravenous appetites and unearned righteousness. That afternoon, the welcoming people asked them to leave. The visitors brandished their rusty weapons and pitiful guns.

The migizi doodem made their report to Gram and the rest of the old ones who made the big decisions. No one said anything because the decision on how to proceed did not need discussion or elaboration. We knew the visitors had seen smoke from the hill and would come after they rested and sobered up. We could already hear drunken war chants below. It was inevitable.

The old ones sent the waabizheshi doodem to take care of the problem.

We walked home after the meeting. We kept quiet and kept the lights off until the next morning.

The village had no choice but to protect us from the savages.

Gram

Parker's Gram loved her very, very much. Two weeks after Parker was born, her mom went back to the office, leaving her daughter with Gram for the day. Gram lived with Uncle and worked nights at the veterans hospital and would be asleep when Parker arrived in the morning. Parker played quietly so as not to wake her. She played with Uncle's old toys—Lincoln Logs, Hot Wheels cars, a train set, an Atari 2600—while he slept in his room, the one with the funny smell and the *Car and Driver* magazines stacked four feet high in the corner. Parker spent her days with Gram until kindergarten, and then, half days.

Parker didn't want to give school a chance. She wanted to stay with Gram and chew on frozen toaster waffles and watch game shows and soaps all day. She and Gram got along just fine, and there was no reason to make a change. Besides, Mr. Tom, her teacher, was mean as a junkyard dog, like the man in her dad's records.

Parker and Gram had been going to camp meetings since before Parker turned five, two or three times a year. They went to Mount Pleasant, Northport, White Pigeon, wherever there were Indians praising Jesus. Parker never cared for sitting around in the outdoor chapels with the woodchip floors, singing and praising the Lord, but she loved playing with her cousins in the woods, getting filthy dirty, and eating fry bread like it was going out of style. A week before kindergarten started, Parker jumped off the monkey bars from the top rung (hey, everyone else was doing it) and broke a small bone in her foot. The pain was almost ticklish, and Parker loved the idea of being hobbled, getting a cast and crutches, and receiving loads of extra attention and sympathy. Instead, she got a brace; she got yelled at by her new teacher for being slow and got her gram in trouble with her mom.

Parker could not hide her disappointment with school. Even at five, she decided her childhood glory days were over. School was the beginning of growing up, responsibility, getting a job someday. She hadn't met anyone that liked their job. It wasn't anything to look forward to. Afternoons and then summer brought some relief, back to the days staying with Gram, sitting with her as she knitted and watched the tube or read, helping her cook and clean, polishing her nurse's shoes, and writing her checks out for her. Her arthritis twisted her knuckles and writing was a terrible chore.

First grade was worse because Parker had to attend school all day. She explained to her parents that she had believed school only needed to be half-day—all the kids did in class in the afternoons was take naps and watch *Sesame Street*. She could definitely do that at home. Her parents would not relent so she punished them by not making friends, not taking naps, and not trying very hard in school. She still saw Gram on weekends and even spent the night on Saturdays. One weekend, during a thorough woman-to-woman talk, Gram explained that she should not blame her parents for school. Her parents would go to jail if she didn't go to school and try harder. Parker didn't know that. Had she known that earlier, she would have gone without complaint, no matter how ridiculous she considered school.

After first grade, Gram retired from the vets, and Parker spent all summer with her in the red 1973 Chevy Nova going to camp meetings. She started second grade with a better attitude and made friends and played nice with the other kids at recess. In class, she finished her assignments in half the time as other students and had the time to read more books. On weekends, she played Scrabble with Gram, starting with the junior version, then quickly switched to the one without words already spelled out on the board. Often, cousins and aunts would come over on Saturday nights for iced tea, potato chips, and Scrabble. They'd bring a cheap, plastic hourglass timer and a dictionary over and played to win. If it wasn't in the dictionary or you took too long, you had to pass. Parker still did well, at least until it got too late for her to stay awake.

Retired, Gram started gaining weight and did more visiting. She loved Spanish rice, hamburg deluxes, strawberry shortcake, lemon meringue pie, bean burritos with extra onions, and all kinds of nuts.

In the summer after fourth grade, Parker's mom stopped leaving her daughter at Gram's. She allowed her daughter to sleep in and get herself over to Gram's. Gram lived only a few blocks away behind the ice cream place on Adams Street. Parker and Gram fought a lot that summer, especially when Parker slept in until nine thirty or ten and wouldn't answer the phone when Gram called. Parker started reading more adult books, books her dad liked: Peter Straub, Stephen King, Elmore Leonard, and so on. She hid these books from Gram. Gram was a religious woman and wouldn't approve of horror stories with a ton of swears and badly depicted sex scenes. On weekends (and weekdays she could get away with it), she stayed up late watching the movie channels and MTV. She and Gram watched the *Martian Chronicles* miniseries over ice cream, popcorn, Spanish rice leftovers, marshmallows, and hamburg deluxes or bean burritos with extra onions from the bar and grill down the street.

When Parker turned twelve, Gram took her out to Peshawbestown to teach her how to drive. She warned Parker to keep it from her parents and since Parker and Gram had always kept secrets since before Parker could remember, it was no problem and very exciting. Gram's dad made her drive him all over the place as soon as she turned twelve, so he could read on the way. By then, Gram drove a blue 1979 Chevy Nova with air conditioning. She was shorter and had to look through the space beneath the top of the steering wheel and the dash to see the road. She never, ever got into accidents but always drove fast, at least until Parker took a curve on Setterbo Road a little too fast. A lot of Indians had died on that road, so she drove slower so as to stop influencing Parker the wrong way.

When Parker was fourteen, she drove Gram to the last camp meeting they'd attend. That one was in Mount Pleasant, the same place she had broken her foot nearly ten years earlier. Parker allowed herself to overload on nostalgia and really understood for the first time that her gram would not live forever. She was inconsolable, and Gram let her stay the whole time in the Holiday Inn to eat greasy chicken nuggets, watch bad made-for-TV movies, and listen to Elton John's "Goodbye Yellow Brick Road."

When Parker received her learner's permit the next summer, Gram took advantage, making Parker drive her all over the state. They visited uncles in Flint and Allegan, aunts in Ypsilanti and Kalamazoo, cousins in Battle Creek and Hopkins and Dorr. They went to tribal council meetings in Dowagiac and pow wows all over the place, every weekend it seemed. Gram was more of a camp meeting woman, but that summer she wanted to try all the different kinds of fry bread at all the different pow wows to see if any of them compared to her sister's fry bread. None did. In Dowagiac, she showed Parker the picture of the Pokagon tribal council hanging on the wall. It was dated 1929. Gram pointed out that the gaunt man on the far left was her father. When Parker was in college, Congress published that photograph in one of its documents when it recognized the Pokagon Band for good. The photo proved that the Pokagons had never given up, unlike so many other tribes.

At the end of the summer, right before school started, Gram asked Parker where she wanted to go. Parker had been driving her around all summer, and it was Parker's turn to choose where they went. Parker knew that Gram wanted to go to the camp meeting way down by White Pigeon, so Parker suggested they go there. Gram said that was fine, and they hit the road. As they entered Grand Rapids on US 131, Gram asked Parker if she really wanted to go to an old camp meeting or if she would rather stop at the new hotel on Pearl Street and spend the night there—order pizza, watch TV, savoring the cool air conditioning, and swim in the pool. Parker chose the hotel.

When Parker turned eighteen, Gram stopped driving altogether. She could no longer see over the dash and gave the car to one of Parker's cousins in Hopkins. Gram started taking strong pain medication—one level below morphine—and nitro capsules for her heart just to get her through the day. The new meds must have changed her mental picture because she started talking about her childhood, her young adulthood years before she got married, and her family. Before, she rarely spoke of those times and people, the heartache too great. She took drops because her eyes were dry, but she always told Parker it was because she had cried until all of her tears had run out. She began remembering Indian words that the sisters had made her forget at the boarding school her father sent her to when her mom died giving birth to Aunt Louise. She talked about the religious schools in North Dakota and Indiana where she worked in her twenties. She talked about how she had been a powder-puff champion race car driver, touring all over Michigan until her dad made her stop, made her come home to help with her younger sisters. She talked about the brothers and sisters that had walked on ahead of her, some of them gone forty or fifty years by then. She even talked about her husband, Parker's grandfather, Ben. He was charming and very, very smart, dangerously so. He liked to drink and gamble and never took his responsibilities as a husband and father seriously. She loved him and always had, forgiving him for his transgressions, but avoided him like the plague from the day he left for the last time because she knew that she would always take him back, again and again, no matter how much he broke her heart.

When she came home from college, Parker always stopped first at Gram's place to have a hamburg deluxe or a bean burrito with extra onions. Gram usually slipped Parker a few twenties when Parker stepped in to visit from college in Mount Pleasant. School is expensive, she'd say, and it would make her feel better to know that her oldest granddaughter had a couple of dollars in her jeans if she wanted to see a show or order a hamburg deluxe.

When Parker came home pregnant, Gram was the first family member she told, and the only one to get excited right away. Parker's mom didn't talk about it for a week until Gram reminded her that her own daughter also had come home unmarried and pregnant twenty years earlier, so she better be nice about it.

And yet Gram scolded Parker harshly when Parker refused to bring her boyfriend, Strickland, home, making Parker cry for two hours straight. Gram underestimated her power and joined in the weeping when she realized how much she had injured her precious granddaughter in a time of uncertainty. In her eighth month, Parker finally brought Strickland to Gram's apartment behind the ice cream place on Adams Street and, after sharing a Coke and a game of Scrabble, took him over to her mom's house.

A few weeks later, Gram, Parker, and Strickland were playing Scrabble over hamburg deluxes when Parker's water broke. By then, Gram could get around her little apartment okay, but she needed a wheelchair and an oxygen tank to move around outside. Gram implored them to leave her and get to Northport, but Parker insisted that Strickland help Gram put on her coat, hook up her oxygen, and wheel her out to the car. Parker's mom made it to the hospital a half-hour before they did as a result. Hours later, Strickland took the first picture, Gram sitting in her chair holding the baby boy, Niko, with the new mom and new Gramma nearby.

Parker brought the boy over to Gram's every day for a little while, whenever she and Strick needed a break. Gram didn't change too many diapers for her great-grandchild, but she did speak exclusively in Indian to him when they were alone, a much more difficult task.

Gram started needing oxygen all the time a few months after the boy was born. She got out of doors less and less and became crankier. Parker's mom did all her laundry and cleaned her up when necessary. Parker hated to do it, but she moved downstate to go back to school in the fall. Parker called her Gram twice a week but could rarely afford the gas money to come home on weekends. Gram often spoke of being lonely, that she was tired of living and had seen and met everyone she had wanted to meet. She kept saying it was time.

The last conversation Parker had with her gram was on a Tuesday. Gram told her that she wanted to go to Heaven to see her dad and brothers and sisters. Parker said to wait a little while longer, not knowing what else to say. "Wait until Niko has to start kindergarten, Gram." Gram always gave the best explanations to talk kids into doing the things they didn't want to do. The explanations usually involved jail and a flyswatter.

Gram said she would try but would make no promises. She did ask Parker if Parker had actually believed the threat of jail all those times. Parker never answered because she was crying too hard.

Gram waited several minutes until her granddaughter calmed down. Finally, she said, "Well, granddaughter, I don't think I can wait that long."

"You better try," Parker said.

Gram walked on a few days later. After the wake, Parker and her family drove went to the bar and grill down the street and ordered hamburg deluxes and bean burritos with extra onions.

My Father Was in Jail Again

My father was in jail again, and I called around to see if any of my former bondsman buddies would cut him a break if I vouched for him. I didn't have a lot of faith in those people, or my father for that matter.

When my dad first called me eight years ago, when I was lifting a lot of weights, drinking a lot of Andre Cold Duck, and working as a special assistant to Larry Livingston, a bail bondsman. I didn't even know who he was because I hadn't seen him since I was three and he had dropped the name Anthony something-Navajo-sounding. I only noticed him because he was carrying a couple knives and a wad of cash that would have gotten Chile out of hock. Plus, he kept looking at me and making me nervous. He knew who I was and had gone in there on purpose, to set me up. He was buying a bond on a fellow named Richardson, a former minor-league shortstop and big-time fixer. And also a thief.

I had been told my father's name was Lenny Price, but that was as untrue as the name he used that day. I eventually learned that my father had several names. He had fourteen social security numbers and accompanying passports, seven of which he had never used. They were reserves. He had more driver's licenses than could be counted and more credit cards than any one person would ever need. He didn't even use them. He just had them.

"Just a lie to back up a lie," my father would say. "If anyone checks, there's something there."

I've still never learned my father's given name, his real name. He chuckled when I asked. "Do you really think my name is important? A name is a chain, a leash, a tag, so people can keep track of you, demean you when it suits them, restrict you to one singular person, personality." He always talked like that, rambling.

"So what do I call you?" I asked.

"Call me father," he'd say. "Call me dad. That's what I am. Your dad. Daddio."

That kept me quiet. My dad was a smart man, albeit a man with no conscience or sense about right and wrong. He made a lot of money being nobody; he knew all the cracks in the system. He wasn't a violent man, for the most part. Violence is the last refuge of the desperate and all that happy-crappy. He would talk for hours and hours, talking like a teacher. Like Jesus, even. We'd all listen, and he was very persuasive. I tended to believe everything he said. He got me into some very deep holes and would hoist me out of them very easily, as easily as lifting a baby out of a crib. And then hand me ten grand for my trouble. I wanted to love him but he wasn't a man that love would ever touch. He was the polar opposite. I thought he was the devil.

We were at a diner a couple months after he came back to me. I told him no.

He looked up at me and blew smoke at the server a half mile away. "No, what?"

"I'm no fuckin' thief."

My old man laughed. "How do you know? You're not even twenty-one. You still got fuckin' acne all over your face."

I blushed mightily. That was a low blow. My dad was king of low blows. "I know who I am." My mother talking.

"So do I," my old man said. "So do I. You're me. You're my flesh and blood, and one thing I learned about DNA and genetic engineering is that the sociopath gene and the klepto gene come directly from the father's side of the family." My father spoke directly to the point. "It's in the Y chromosome. Heh-heh. Trust me, son."

"I don't want to get caught, to go to jail." I was reduced to whining, as all parents eventually reduce their children.

"Stick with me," he said as grave and death. "You'll never get caught if you stick with me."

I walked out of the diner without paying for my coffee and drove off before my father could see me cry.

I hadn't seen or heard from my dad in eight years when he called me from the county lock-up again. This time he said his name was Abel Lombardi, but I recognized his voice. It's like he knew I would, and I could almost see him wink as he said the name. As I called around for a bondsman, I kept thinking that getting arrested was his way of life, or maybe just for getting attention. Our conversation was brief—the two-minute limit in effect—but it was long enough for him to tell me he thought my maintenance and plant management job was a joke.

I remembered mentioning once over beers to my friends that my old man could get away with a whole lotta shit by shifting identities. At the time, thinking a whole lotta shit couldn't amount to much more than bankruptcy, I said, "You could charge up one of these credit cards, buy a bunch of stuff, and walk away. You'd get all that stuff, and no one would know who you are." Hell, I remembered thinking, I'm his son and I didn't even know who he was.

What had "Abel Lombardi" done to get landed this time around? My dad told me before that he needed me to help keep him free, to avoid the clink. "Working alone is a slow death," he said. "Just a matter of time."

I cursed my dad for messing with me. I needed him all those years, and he just wanted me for an heir to a criminal fortune of credit cards and empty overseas bank accounts I could never touch. Plus, I'd eat the bond and my name would be mud around town because my pop was still my pop, and he would morph into some other criminal identity.

I opened a bottle of my favorite brand of malt liquor, the one with the cartoon Indian on the bottle, and proceeded to do some serious thinking. I called my former employer, Larry, and told him the truth. He was used to it. Larry was the best and would be able to track "Abel" and bring him in for the trial. Professionals like Larry didn't enjoy the extra work. I offered twenty percent instead of the usual ten and told him what to expect.

The next thing I did was change my phone number and delist.

Boss Gorton

Boss Gorton sat in his office in the big house letting the sun go down, the light sliding away, sliding down the roof and out toward the trees, melting into the woods like a predator. Quiet. Loitering. He puffed on his last stogie, the smoke drifting into the still, humid air, draped over him like a shroud of Turin. The room turned darker, darker, until it drifted away like an old, forgotten argument. The books on the shelves faded away with history, the chairs in the room like ash. Like the sanity of a soldier trapped in a vertical tube of mutually assured destruction or the homeless freed and warmed by unlabeled hooch. The safe stayed put. A man standing in the doorway, illuminated by the white paint covering the walls in the big house, standing for almost five hundred years, finally able to stop.

"Will there be anything else, Boss?" Steven the butler asked.

"No, thank you." A long pause. Uncomfortable silence, like the moment after an unexpected break-up. They both wanted to not look at each other, but they couldn't step away. "I'll bet you'll be glad to take those stupid-lookin' whites off."

"Yessir." Steven wasn't going to let the old man float away. He held his breath and listened to the silence, pulling the house and its master down like a million, billion-ton anchor, a purgatorial slippery slope. Then, the old man spoke.

"Well, this is it. You have anything to say, say it now." Boss turned to Steven and, for the first time since Steven's job interview twelve years ago, looked him in the eyes.

Steven hesitated. He thought about everything that had happened. Too much, too much that mattered, too much payback. There still was darkness at the end of the tunnel, but someone had spotted a dove. Finally, he looked back at Boss and said, "I had a little speech prepared, but it seems so . . . nothing. All I can think of to say now is no life raft can save us now." And with that, Steven executed one of those perfect turns for the last time and walked out the house, smiling. Boss watched him go.

Ungrateful bastard, Boss thought. After all I did for him. Treated him with respect. Was generous to his family. Insults me in my own home. This world deserves all this.

Boss waited until the sun was down and it was almost dark to get into his last rig, a used 1981 Ford pickup. Everything he needed was packed into the cab in an efficient pattern. He started up the rusted-out black truck and pulled away from his $11 million mansion, swimming pool, personal golf course, shooting range, and all the rest. It was a beautiful home, a castle, like in the feudal times. He considered himself the local nobility. The residents of the parish were poor as peasants in fourteenth-century Europe. The place stank of poverty, but he was glad to be king of something. Pointless. He was nothing now, just like everyone else—a damn commoner. He rolled the window down and smelled the fresh, evening air for what seemed like forever. Louisiana air, for all its pollution and sweat, had rare moments of purity and cleanliness Boss would miss.

Boss was alone on the road. Most everyone in these parts could not afford a vehicle or the gun like the one Boss kept in the glove compartment. He felt poor and used and washed-up, but he was still the richest man around. No one was there to help him. No one to change his mind. No one to stop him. Alone.

The truck rattled over the cracked and worn pavement. No one would see fit to fix this road again, Boss thought. Not anymore. Sure as hell not the Indians. Boss's truck was damn near full with gasoline, fuel that had a value of about a billion spacebucks, in 2025 dollars. No one had use for gas anymore, and Boss could not use the money even if he could manage to sell the gas.

Boss paid no heed to the road signs. He drove fast and then slow, weaving all over the road, relishing his blatant disregard for public safety. There was no public anymore. He would not have to stop or yield. There were no people to run over or sideswipe. There were no cars out here, and, if there were, so what? No pigs, either. It made Boss think of the old days, when he truly was Boss, and no one would dare cross him. He did anything he wanted, and no one ever said boo. Times had changed. The parish that he owned dried up like a fall leaf. The color, the vision, the community. All dead, gone, driven away by bad government, crime, lack of jobs. His life as the local baron degenerated as the parish wrinkled and wasted away.

Boss turned on his tape deck with Hank Williams the elder. Boss pretended he was listening to it for the first time, fifty-odd years ago. Tears welled up in his eyes, and they sparkled with the light from the embers on the side of the road where the few people who were left burned their most precious and valuable possessions. Even out here, where some of the poorest people in Louisiana lived, there were some valuable things. Objects had value once. The only value to people here now was the ability to burn something, to ensure that no one else got it.

After a few more minutes, as the sun went down, Boss recovered some of the hardness he had when he was in charge and pressed the accelerator down further. He was close now and was getting anxious. Soon, he would be home. No time for feelings. He turned down the narrow lane that led to his original family home, the place he had been conceived and born in. A place he had left over sixty years earlier and had not seen with his own eyes since. He was not even sure it was here after all this time.

And then, there it was.

The house, a weathered old shack even the hungriest termites had left to rot, stood in open space. Boss's father had cut all the trees down on this forty-acre proverbial lot and built the house—it was a real house then—over the stumps. Boss left the headlights on and rummaged around for his lantern and a flashlight. He wanted to get a good look around first.

The house had only two rooms, a big one and a small one, where his parents slept. Boss took a look and lit a match, preparing to throw it on some old curtains and furniture.

"Hello, son," Boss's mother said, as if she had been waiting decades for this time alone with him.

Boss turned and saw his mother, who was dead. She looked good for a woman who had given birth to nine children, if a bit thin.

"Hello, mother," Boss answered. He was not very surprised to see her, even if she was a ghost. Nowadays, there were ghosts everywhere, like an epidemic.

"We didn't have much, did we?" his mother mused. "But we were happy."

Boss did not respond, and they were silent for some time. He knew he was caught in the act.

"I was always proud of you, son. I know you did your best, and you got what you wanted. I wish I could hold you and make it all better again." Then she was gone.

No "I love you's."

Boss waited until sunrise to burn down his childhood home and shoot himself in the head. He always had that good special feeling at dusk and at dawn.

Sarah's Sister

Violet played well. Sarah watched her from the back of the smoky room of the place the *Village Voice* had complimented more for the strength of its drinks than for the guest musicians. Sarah could see Violet focusing on the music, giving it more attention than that place deserved. While Violet stroked the keys with tenderness, in complete control of the instrument in front of her, Sarah felt angry for a moment that few in the bar seemed to notice her sister's grace, her talent. They were there to drink, to converse, to strike deals, and to show off their expensive work clothes, the suits with the tailored silk and the perfect color schemes. Sarah sipped her martini, a rare luxury and a concession to the place (posted on the door: "two drink minimum"). She saw Violet pause for a perfect moment while she chose another piece. Violet played without urgency or, it appeared, the need to be praised. She played for herself and a small stipend, Sarah suspected. Violet was an artist with a decent paying gig. Few artists could hope even for such a modest career, as Sarah's own continued failed attempts at selling her sculptures attested. Sarah wondered if there were Odawakwewaag anywhere near this bar, more Odawa women Sarah could bring in the door and say, "That's my sister over there. She's a reasonably successful musician, making a living playing piano in New York City." She wanted to brag about her sister, a woman she had never met, a woman that scared her.

Sarah found Violet eleven months earlier.

Sarah grew up in Santa Fe, the adopted daughter of a gray-haired Caucasian violinist with long-term career aspirations. Beth had wanted a daughter but didn't want to take the time off from her full-time orchestral work to waste nine and a half months with a baby inside her. And she wanted a Native child because in the early 1970s Santa Fe social scene to which she subscribed, having an Indian child was akin to being royalty. Beth never even knew or cared which kind of Indian her daughter would be, just as long as she was potty-trained and could help out around the house.

On some days (and in some dreams, the rare ones where everyone spoke Anishinaabemowin), Sarah could make out her biological mother's face—and she could make out the faces of her brother and sisters. They were all just toddlers when the Antrim County social workers came for them.

Beth made her sit through art classes at the Indian center and learn the bumbling intricacies of liberal politics by watching the Democratic national conventions of the Mondale and Dukakis eras. And she wasn't allowed to invite any of the other Indian kids, mostly Navajos and Pueblo Indians, to the house for slumber parties, even when she promised to clean up. Her only friends were her mother's friends' children. When she left for college, Berkeley, Sarah gave up on Beth and started looking for her mom and her siblings. The search took more time and effort than normal because Sarah refused to ask Beth for information, refused to even mention it. She didn't want the woman to know. By then, Sarah just referred to Beth as "the woman"—the woman who raised her, she said to her friends, the woman who took her away from her family, she said privately and to her therapist. When she learned she was a Michigan Odawa woman (officially, a potential member of the Grand River Band of Ottawa Indians), she was slightly disappointed. She wanted to be Navajo or Chiricahua Apache, something exotic, with a heritage of war parties and marketable artistry. After a few months of investigation, her tribe's membership coordinator informed her that her biological mother had passed away in 1980. So she looked for her siblings.

Sarah found her brother in San Pedro, California. He had changed his name to Ramon Elias and was singing and playing bass for a punk rock group called The Idjit Children. She subscribed to the *LA Weekly* from her place in Oakland and watched for notices that his band would be playing in LA somewhere. She drove down to see him twice. Both times she couldn't approach him. She thought he was a pig. He drank and swore at the audience. He was abusive and made sexist comments on stage. He bragged about his dick piercings. She wanted to love him, to approach him and tell him the truth about his background, that he was a Michigan Odawa man and he could have a real family. She didn't; she left him alone. Maybe he didn't need or want to know about how he used to cry all night, keeping his sisters awake all night, nights when they were all so lonely. She wanted to remember him as a baby, innocent and forever Odawa.

Sarah found her other sister in Seattle. Her new name was Mary Childress, and she was a music teacher in the Fremont neighborhood. She had four children of her own, and they looked like beautiful Odawa babies. She was a widow. Sarah learned from visiting the library that her husband had contracted HIV/AIDS from a hospital needle before there were adequate controls. Sarah took four trips to Seattle in her beaten-down Honda Civic to meet her oldest sister, the one she remembered being the tiny boss of the family when their mother disappeared from their lives. She observed her from across the street while Mary watched the kids playing on an asphalt playground at their elementary school. She saw Mary go into the video store with her four daughters to rent the latest cartoons. She saw Mary shop for musical instruments she couldn't afford on a music teacher's salary, and she watched while Mary perused books on her favorite musicians in the Fremont bookstore. In the end, Sarah decided that Mary's life was already complete even with its flaws and the last thing her sister needed was another family member to disrupt her life.

Sarah moved to Brooklyn when she graduated. She had been accepted at a lower Manhattan art school. She forgot about her siblings, about the search for her family. She would still receive the tribe's newsletter in the mail every month, and she felt a twinge about giving up but did nothing about it. She found Violet purely by accident, seeing her in a coffee shop, reading a trade magazine for professional musicians. She saw Violet, and it was like looking in a mirror. It scared her to see this woman that looked exactly like her but with shorter hair and better clothes. She followed

Violet. She followed her to a smoky bar that featured live music. She watched the show that first night and promised herself that she would approach her after. And again another night a month later. And again another night four months later.

Sarah turned back to her martini. She wasn't a drinker—too much in her family had been ruined by drink—and the two sips she had taken went straight to her head. She couldn't focus on the music any longer and didn't notice when it ended. Before she knew it, Violet had sat down right next to her and ordered an iced tea.

"Good to see you again, sister," Violet said to Sarah without emotion, almost like she was pissed off.

Sarah could only stare.

Violet produced a cigarette, and the bartender lit it for her. "I'm sorry about the smoking, but I've been in these bars so long that I can't help it."

"How long?" Sarah stammered.

"Since I was a young woman, I guess." Violet smiled and took a long drag. The bartender nodded at her, giving her some sort of signal, and then moved away. "Are you really my sister? I mean, you look like me. That's what Isaac said last time you were here, and I tell ya, I can't disagree."

Sarah began to cry a little. "Yes, I think so. We're twins."

"I know," Violet said. "I remember you, you know." She took and long drag, held it, and let the smoke draft from her mouth. "I thought we would be best friends our whole lives, even then. What happened?"

"It happened to all of us," Sarah said. She looked down.

Violet put out her cigarette. "I'm so glad you're here," she said, her voice cracking a little, finally emotional. "I'm so alone here. There aren't many Indians in Manhattan. And even if there were . . ." She put her face in her sister's shoulder.

Sarah wanted to know everything about Violet right then—where she had been taken after they had all been split up; if she had been adopted or transferred from foster home to foster home; how and where she learned to play; who had abused her; everything—but the woman, who wasn't exactly weeping on her shoulder, wasn't talking right then. Sarah could wait to hear everything. There was plenty of time.

The Chain Gangs

"Did you hear about the new guy?"

Prevo looked up from his mopping. "No. Where is that lazy bastard? Hung over again?"

Summer squinted, annoyed with her coworker. "No." She looked around the coffee shop to see if anyone was looking at them, listening. "He was attacked last night. He has two broken ribs, and they had to wire his jaw shut."

Prevo whistled and said holy shit before Summer touched him on the arm to make him quiet down.

"That's awful," Prevo said, almost whispering. "Why are we so quiet about it?"

"A few friends of mine who work for the Mongolian Barbecue have been acting strange lately. They're starting to wear their black polo shirts all the time, not just at work. My roommate Teena, who works at Blimpy Burger on Packard . . ."

"Cheaper than food?"

"Yeah. She's been harassed on the street by Applebee's and Outback Steakhouse employees."

"Uh-huh. Whatever. I call bullshit on you."

Prevo annoyed Summer, the way he talked with all the college bohemian style of the mid-1990s, but he was the only guy who didn't hit on her all the time. “No, I’m serious. She says those guys wear their green or whatever polo shirts all the time, too, and they hang out together on street corners. Almost like hoods from Flatbush in the fifties. Or the Warriors.”

Rocky, one of the sandwich specialists, walked over. “You talking about those chain restaurant people? The Mongolian Barbecue thing? I’ve been seeing them in the alley behind their restaurant standing in a circle holding hands and chanting. They’re like some sort of cult.”

Prevo thought for a second. “You know, I’ve been seeing a lot of those Macaroni Grill people down at the mall, acting tough and laughing at people. It’s kinda intimidating.”

Summer said it first, “They’re forming gangs. It’s only a matter of time before they start fighting over turf. Maybe it’s already started.”

Prevo looked out the front window and saw four Mongolian Barbecue employees wearing their black polo shirts. They were just standing there, staring at them through the window. Prevo made sure not to make eye contact, got back to work, and tried not to think about it.

Over the next few weeks, Summer noticed more changes. The end of August came and went, and more graduate students patronized the Main Street Rema’s store, just like every year Summer had worked there since graduating from the university. She started seeing Applebee’s employees wandering around her neighborhood near State, Packard, and Hill Streets. Some of them had begun carrying baseball bats. Some wore green bandanas and engineer boots. Her roomie, Teena, quit her job at Blimpy’s, tired of seeing Outback Steakhouse employees coming inside and making a huge, threatening racket, overturning chairs and scaring the customers and the workers. The management had called the police a few times, but they always arrived way too late. The owner talked about closing down for the fall—the high point of the undergraduate burger season—to see if things would cool down.

Prevo had seen some Mongolian Barbecue employees carrying bats, and some wore handsome leather knife sheaths on their belts like urban Daniel Boones. He walked to work every day from his rented house in the Old West neighborhood near Seventh and West Washington. His housemates, both sixth-year English undergraduates, reported scuffles at frat parties involving McDonald’s and Burger King employees. He heard rumors that some frats were considering aligning themselves with fast-food chains to avoid drunken brawls, fires, and other dangers at their weekend parties.

Rocky came into work one day with a black eye and a cut on his left earlobe. He had stitches. Rema's management sent him home, unhappy that their finest sandwich specialist had open cuts and ugly bruises on his face and head. Prevo ran outside as Rocky left, tucking his Rema's badge in his backpack.

"What happened, Rocky?"

Rocky winced and looked around. Prevo had seen a lot of his friends do that in the last few days, suffering from paranoia, thinking someone might be listening or watching. He looked like a frightened schoolchild on a poorly lit, inner-city, gang-infested street corner though it was only ten o'clock on a fine, sunny Ann Arbor morning. "Those barbecue people caught up to me last night coming back from the movies. There was about six or seven. I don't know. Only a couple of them were guys. The dudes held me down, and then these women started pounding on me. They ripped out my earring. My mom gave me that earring."

"What did the police say?"

"Man, I ain't gonna talk to no police. They've got other things to do than help out a bunch of loser twentysomething wage slaves."

Prevo nodded. "Lemme give you a ride home. We gotta stick together now."

Rocky shook his head. "No, I can travel better alone. I've been living here a long time, and I know a few places to hide, a few tricks. Stay here."

"Well, okay. Later."

Summer was alarmed after Prevo told her about Rocky's injuries. "What am I going to do now? If I quit then, I'll lose my apartment. If I don't, Grizzly Peak and Jolly Pumpkin stooges will smear me all over the road."

Prevo nodded. "Call the boys who live in that house on Greenwood. Tell them to get every Rema's employee we know to show up at their place tonight after close. We need to organize for our own safety."

About fifteen people showed up at Greenwood, five from each of the three Rema's stores in Ann Arbor. As the meeting began, Jimmie and Lola, a married couple who doubled as engineering grad students and managers at the Church Street location, were telling everyone about the

Taco Bell on East University that had just gone up in smoke minutes earlier.

"Grease fire?" someone asked, a nervous twitter in her voice.

"Could be," Jimmie said, meaning that it couldn't be. He was the oldest employee at the gathering, his wife a few years younger. Most of the Rema's people there were between eighteen and twenty-two, with a sprinkling of them a few years older, like Summer.

Prevo stood and called the meeting to order. "That Taco Bell thing means the stakes are higher now. I just got back from the library downtown looking at the police beat columns from the last few weeks of the *Ann Arbor News*. There's been a rash of muggings and random assaults of people walking home from work. I bet most of the victims worked for local restaurants and coffee shops. I think what we all know now is that chain restaurant workers have been terrorizing people like us."

"Are you saying the Pizza Hut slash Taco Bell slash KFC slash Pepsi people will go after . . . I dunno . . . Applebee's and Outback Steakhouse people now?" someone asked.

"Maybe. Actually, I hope so."

"I hate those Applebee's fuckers," Linda, a State Street manager, said.

"Anyway," Prevo said, trying to keep the meeting on his agenda, "we all admit we know what we're facing."

"But why?" Linda asked. "What's going on?"

Summer chipped in. "The corporation makes them act like a family. Hell, our own families didn't even act like families. They can't work anywhere else, so they start buying into the fake corporate family mentality. Some of the corporations actually call their lowest-level workers 'front-line employees' like the army or something."

"Well, that's us, too," a woman from the State Street store said. "Why aren't we turning into goons?"

Jimmie smiled. "Well, we're here now, aren't we? Aren't we turning into gang right now?"

Prevo shook his head. "No, we'll never be a gang. We do this for protection, for understanding. We need our jobs. We're not in it for the turf or the action."

A guy who lived at the Greenwood house and worked at the State Street store said, "A lot of people are quitting."

Prevo snapped. “Those are just students. They can get away with unemployment. I, for one, need my job. I don’t go to school on the public dole, and I ain’t no quitter.”

“Me, either!” someone said.

“Damn right!” someone else said.

Summer nodded her head and felt more secure than she had in weeks, like maybe they’d make it through this.

The group agreed to talk to the other Rema’s employees who couldn’t make it and set up scheduled trips in small groups to and from work at each of the three locations.

That evening, Summer felt so confident about her job security situation that she talked Teena into applying at Rema’s.

Prevo drove over to Rocky’s apartment on North Division after the meeting. They talked late into the night about security. They each agreed to apply for concealed weapons permits. Neither had a criminal record of any kind, and they figured they had nothing to lose.

The fire at the East University Taco Bell burned with unusual fury due to some strange chemicals the Ann Arbor Fire Department hadn’t seen before, and they were unable to respond when the Chi-Chi’s on State Street, south of I-94, exploded at midnight. A student editorial jokingly referred to the gassy content of the beans at both restaurants, glossing over the fact that two chain restaurants had been torched within a matter of hours.

Over the next month, the violence between the chain restaurants and coffee shops escalated. Two Starbucks shops were trashed and defiled. Rumor indicated that Starbucks workers had retaliated by firebombing the Big Boy at Briarwood and the Old Country Buffet on Eisenhower. New Starbucks shops sprung up within days, and green-clad Starbucks berserkers began patrolling the mall.

On Main Street, the Mongolian Barbecue mob upped their own patrols, beefing up their numbers and weaponry. Their black-and-yellow-shirted soldiers seemed less human than the others, more brainwashed and trained in psychological terror. They never seemed to nurse injuries like the other chain gangs.

Over this period of time, the Rema’s employees noted a considerable drop in harassment from the various chain restaurant gangs. Prevo claimed the security measures they had adopted at the Greenwood meeting (he called it the "Greenwood Protocol") were effective. Summer thought otherwise.

"Maybe they're worried about Starbucks," she said to Prevo one day.

"No way," Prevo said. "There's no place for Starbucks to get a foothold downtown. Everything's filled up."

"Ah, but if Mongolian Barbecue got greedy and took out one of the smaller, local stores, then maybe Starbucks could fill the void, build a foothold, and swarm in like locusts. Look at South University. Look at Main Street. Packard. State Street."

"That's a good point. We're no real threat to the blackshirts, so they leave us alone. And we serve a purpose, a buffer of sorts for the barbecue people from outside intervention and influence. It's almost like we have a get out of jail free card. We have a form of immunity."

"Maybe." Summer thought that was dangerous and dubious logic.

Prevo never mentioned his concealed weapon—an old Glock 17 his grandfather gave him—and neither did Rocky mention his own weapon. They had become the unofficial masters of security, ferrying Rema's workers to and from work, even at night. On breaks, they'd discuss how the conflict between the chain restaurants proceeded.

"Ben and Jerry's is done for," Rocky reported one day. "They're such hippies, even after being bought out by that big corporation. They all got jumped by the Applebee's people yesterday, and their store was looted."

"And I heard the Big Boy at the Ann Arbor–Saline complex was torched," Prevo said. "The Elias Brothers must be crying in their strawberries."

The men laughed like grizzled old veterans.

Prevo said, "This war's gonna end someday, maybe someday real soon." He was imagining himself to be Patrick Swayze in *Red Dawn*. "We have to be ready, you know. They'll come for us then."

Rocky nodded. "What do you think we should do?"

"Well, we already have a sort of command structure. We should solidify it, internalize it into the membership, and establish it for the three stores, so everyone knows. Like the old Roman legions they talked about in the *Godfather* movies."

"*The Godfather*?"

"Exactly. You and I will be the capos. And maybe that Jimmie guy. He's a realist. Summer's smart. We need her planning ability. She sees the big picture. She could be the counselor, our consigliore."

"Jimmie works over at the Church Street location, right?"

"Yeah. We'd need someone else we can trust to be a capo at the State Street location. That's the biggest store, the most employees, the most at risk."

"What about that girl Linda?" Rocky suggested. "She's tough and smart, too."

Prevo agreed. "I'll talk to her. You talk to Jimmie. Tell them they'll need a concealed weapons permit. We'll all need one sooner or later."

Summer needed plenty of persuasion when Prevo approached her about his restructuring plan.

"This whole thing was about safety. I don't want to become an armed gang like those corporate animals out there."

Prevo persisted. "Listen, Summer. We need you. Without you behind the scenes, we'll probably become what you hate. You're the only one who saw this whole thing happening long before anyone else. We all need you."

Summer had reservations, but she relented.

Over the next few months, Prevo and his capos selected several well-conditioned Rema's employees from each of the three stores and worked with them, turning them into top-notch street soldiers. They outfitted each of them with switchblades and blackjacks and saw fit to have them trained in street fighting.

Summer counseled them all that self-defense was the paramount concern and under no circumstances would the capos order preemptive or retaliatory attacks. And she emphasized that Rema's employees should never engage in offensive activities.

Meanwhile, the war between the chain restaurants and coffee shops reached a point where a finale was inevitable. Starbucks and the two most powerful chain restaurants—Applebee's and McDonald's—formed a triumvirate of violence and power. From Applebee's outpost across the highway, the three launched devastating assaults on the Ann Arbor–Saline and Briarwood-area restaurants. The fires raged for days and, at the end, the Funky Cabal—as they called themselves—controlled Ann Arbor south of Stadium and hailed themselves as victors. Then, the internecine chaos in the areas around the university campus fired up as the exurban conflicts died down.

Prevo and his team concurrently assessed the whole theater of operations, concluding that Starbucks and McDonald's would move first to fortify their already strong presence in the campus areas. The Mongolian Barbecue nestled in their downtown area would see their near-hegemony as a threat, an encirclement, and would likely lash out. The Funky Cabal's rearguard, Applebee's, would then begin attacking Barbecue gangs in force, and the fight for downtown Ann Arbor would begin.

What Summer never envisioned as she helped Prevo and his captains prepare was the Starbucks Corporation's business acumen, their fifth column—and neither had the Mongolian Barbecue. Without any fanfare, Starbucks began to contact coffee shop landlords and offered ridiculous amounts of cash to convince the landlords to break leases and evict their tenants. She warned Prevo that their estimates of preparation time before things ignited would be shortened.

Then, during the first weeks of the semi–Cold War between the Funky Cabal and the Mongolian Barbecue, Summer had other, more pressing concerns. Prevo blew up at her during a meeting of the security committee—him, Summer, and three captains, Linda, Rocky, and Jimmie.

"I don't give a tiny little shit what we promised, Summer!"

"We said we'd never act in an aggressive manner," Summer insisted.

"My dear Summer, the realities have changed. We have some strength, some negotiating power, and we need to exert ourselves a little to make sure everyone knows we are not to be trifled with."

Prevo had proposed buying some simple Rema's T-shirts to wear around town, just to let the chain store players know how many Rema's employees there were. Summer objected on her principled grounds.

"A month ago, I would have agreed with you, Summer," Linda said.

"I'm worried about the domino effect of the situation," Rocky said, a little clumsily, not really certain of the geopolitics but wanting to appear strong.

"It'll be like a tidal wave," Jimmie said, piping in where Rocky left off. "We've always known that the winner or winners would come after us someday. Hell, Summer, you taught us that."

Prevo paced around the room in the shadows. "Yes. Remember that saying? First they came for the gypsies, and I didn't say anything because I wasn't a gypsy. And then they came for the Jews, and I didn't say anything because I wasn't a Jew. And so on. We're going to make a stand at some point. Let's do something to instill a little pride, a little swagger, before it gets ugly. Let's do this while things are fractionated, and no one's ready to move yet. And the Barbecue is so focused on the Funky Cabal, we might be able to surprise them."

Linda agreed, adding, "We're strong now. We've got forty people ready to move, to do anything we ask. They're ready."

Summer felt horrible. "I guess I knew it would come to this. You had the organization first, then the power. And now you have your little consensus, your little junta."

Prevo looked at his friend and coworker with some sense of false sympathy. "I'm sorry, Summer. I guess you're just not with us anymore."

The next day, Summer and Teena quit Rema's and applied for jobs at Tinkleman's. They knew some decent people there and figured it would be easy to get jobs. They were right. Tinkleman's had far fewer employees than Rema's; many of them had left to get in with the Rema's crew. The Tinkleman's people that remained felt it best to stay out of the chain store conflict. The ownership owned the buildings where the main restaurant was located and, despite losing the bread outlet near downtown to Starbucks, maintained a strong and stable market niche and would survive.

A week after quitting Rema's, Summer and Teena received a visit from a woman neither recognized, wearing a Rema's shirt emblazoned with a sinister-looking green frog. The woman said, "A message from Prevo. He suggests you sit this one out." Was that from *Miller's Crossing* or *Brick*? Summer thought. The woman gave Summer a good shove. "I've heard about you, Summer. There'll be plenty more of that if I see you around in the wrong crowd."

Summer said to Teena later that Prevo and his crew had been watching too many gangster movies.

The next day at Tinkleman's, Teena whispered to Summer that Rocky and a few other Rema's workers jumped a small group of Starbucks employees down on North Division. They had put four of them in the hospital.

"It's too late for them now," Summer said.

Now people began defecting from Rema's to join up with Tinkleman's and other local stores. Many of them had shared Summer's view that the Greenwood Protocol should not be extended to create an armed, violent presence on the street. Some had been expelled from the organization for being too meek or delicate.

The conflict between the Funky Cabal and the Mongolian Barbecue began in earnest a month later when several Applebee's employees drove a van loaded with explosives into the Mongolian Barbecue store and destroyed much of the whole block. The Barbecue went underground, staging violent hit-and-run attacks on McDonald's and Starbucks all over campus and conducting huge, impromptu barbecues at secret locations in parks all over the city.

A bit later, Summer learned that Prevo had miscalculated. One of Prevo's spies had discovered plans for a secret Barbecue picnic at Geddes Park. Prevo planned an all-out offensive, but it was a terrible failure. The brutality of the Barbecue shock troops turned out to be real, and they converged on Rocky and Jimmie's crew like murderous, man-eating barracudas. Few of the Rema's attackers escaped unscathed, with most receiving broken bones and vicious puncture wounds from strange Mongolian Barbecue cooking implements. A couple of Rema's workers perished on the field. The elite crew Prevo had worked so hard to establish was efficiently eliminated in only a few minutes by the ultraviolent Barbecue cult.

Days later, Linda made her own terrible error and led her State Street group into a trap set up for her by the Applebee's people. Knowing of her irrational hatred for the franchise, they caused a double agent to inform her of an Applebee's safe house located on Packard. Without notifying Prevo or asking his advice and permission, she set her crew on the safe house. No one ever saw Linda again.

A week later, after missing several days of work, Prevo learned that he had been downsized by the company, which had just been purchased from above by the Starbucks Corporation. Rocky, suffering from permanent injuries in the Geddes raid, was also cut. Jimmie, suffering from a broken ankle and a deep gash in his stomach, was asked to resign his manager position, along with his wife who then left him.

Unemployed and still in shock from the horrible events of his aggressive security campaign, Prevo walked the streets of Ann Arbor for days, almost asking for the marauding chain gangs to set upon him. The Barbecue caught up to him first, and he disappeared into the same black abyss Linda had been lost to before him.

The hot war between the Mongolian Barbecue and the Funky Three cooled off after the destruction of the Rema's crew, and both sides realized that they would not be able to rid themselves of the other. A couple months after the suicide-bombing of the Mongolian Barbecue, the sides reached a peace accord and agreed to run the city's food industry side by side.

The three Rema's stores remained, the name having a certain value even after it became Starbucks property. Rema's employees either put up with the new corporate lordship or got fired. Many of them did well with their new masters. Prevo had prepared them well to be front-line employees.

Tinkleman's continued to thrive in its niche, strong enough to repel the passive-aggressive threats from the chain restaurants but too weak to expand.

Summer and Teena eventually moved out of Ann Arbor to try their luck in Seattle. They got identical jobs at a local coffee palace called How About A Nice Cup of Shut The F*** Up. It was about four doors down from a Starbucks, and, on some days, Summer thought she saw some of their employees stare at her a little bit longer than she liked.

The Sons of Leopold

The pink-faced deputy sheriff placed a legal-size manilla folder on the desk in front of Tom Argos and stepped back, eyes blank and waiting to see what would happen next. The bare interrogation room was full of armed cops, five of them, but deathly quiet. Tom overplayed the solemnity of the moment, staring lasers at the folder. He took a deep breath before he picked it up, taking in deep the smudge smoke, praying his shredded lungs held up. He looked inside. The images on the analog, black-and-white photos struck him full in the face. The woman must have suffered horribly before she died, though Tom was trained as a lawyer and had no basis to know. He struggled to control his emotions. The blood rushed away from his face. He felt cold in his stomach, the verge of vomiting. He made himself breathe evenly, slowly.

"The punishment for this is always the same," Tom said finally, not looking at anyone. "Tie the perpetrator to a tree or a pole in town. Let the women and children do what they want to him over the next four days, the men don't touch him. Let him go at the end."

There was silence. Tom closed the folder. His job was done. He unfolded his long, thin legs, tried to stand and nearly fell. One of the deputies shifted slightly in a move to help Tom, but he righted himself quickly. Still, age was catching up to him.

Sheriff Randy Lee remained seated at the table across from Tom's seat. He was an obese man, with a hard face that somehow projected kindness. Tom guessed that was why the guy got elected again and again. It was winter, but Lee was still wearing a short-sleeved shirt and tie to go with his badges. Tom could see the scratch marks on Lee's forearms, speckles of blood here and there. He imagined all the men in the room had scratch marks all over.

"Miigwetch," Sheriff Lee said. "Baaniimaa'apii." He nodded to the deputy nearest Tom, who left the room with the rest of the other deputies.

"Aho," Tom said to Lee in the lowest, most gravelly voice he could manage. He stood still for a moment, letting his body equalize before he left. The men didn't have anything to say to each other. Tom knew these itchy white men were suspicious of him, even as they deferred to him. He needed to leave before they started asking questions. But first he had to recover his balance.

The deputies had left the interrogation room from the door behind Tom, but Tom had left his things in the room behind Lee. He began walking around the stainless steel table toward where Lee sat staring at the table. As Tom moved past Lee, the old fat man grabbed him roughly by the elbow.

"How do you know all this?"

Tom spoke the prepared response. This challenge from yet another rural sheriff. But they were becoming more frequent, especially compared to the early days when they wordlessly deferred, back when dissent was unthinkable. "I'm fourth degree Midewiwin in the lodge of Makaday Binesi. I've been a tribal judge for twenty-five years or so. And I dream in the language."

Most of the people that confronted Tom didn't know what to make of the dreaming thing when he said it. But this Sheriff Lee seemed to be taken aback. He let go of Tom's arm. The old look of awe Tom had foolishly gotten used to over the years came over Lee's face. "Okay then. Mino Giizhigad."

"Aho," Tom said again. Dreaming in the language signaled complete mastery of Anishinaabemowin, unquestioned fluency, spiritual connection to the Great Spirit or maybe Nanaboozhoo. Someone who dreamed in the language probably grew up speaking in the language and learning the teachings of the real elders. Someone who deserved, who had earned, respect.

Tom was a goddam liar. He didn't dream in the language.

The elder women in the village beat the perpetrator to death the first night. They always did. The women of Tom's generation, what they used to call the Gen Xers, were the most merciless, nihilist people he had ever known.

The perp would have frozen to death tied to that telephone pole anyway.

Tom had the evening to kill. He would leave the town in the morning in his pickup. He stepped outside the hotel. Light snow covered everything he could see, the crystals sparkling. There was no wind, and he could hear the waves of the big lake crashing into the break, off in the dark. Like most towns Tom traveled to, the streetlights in this town were mostly dark. The one in front of the police station across the street worked, though, and Tom watched as the portly sheriff of Delta County worked his way toward him.

"Evening, Sheriff," Tom said.

"Evenin,'" Randy Lee said.

They stepped inside the bar on the ground floor of the hotel without saying anything. Tom was halfway through his pint of brown ale before Lee said anything.

"Sorry for questioning you earlier." Lee was staring at the little square napkin under his own pint, which he cradled in his hand. He pulled it to his mouth and drank deeply.

"No need." And there wasn't. Tom saw that the sheriff wore a thick plaid button down shirt now, long sleeves covering his arms and the scratches.

They sat at the bar, side by side on wooden stools. It could have been the late nineteenth century instead of the mid-twenty-first. Of course, Tom knew that was the intent of the proprietors. There were two men in the corner table by the front window away from the door smoking self-rolled cigarettes.

"Tile floor," Tom said.

Lee grunted. "The lumbermen tried to civilize the place. I'd prefer wood planks. This looks like the floor of the men's."

Tom did, too, but said nothing.

"I used to drink Miller Lite," Lee said. "Hated those microbrews. Craft beer. Whatever they fuckin' called it."

Tom nodded, taking another sip of the local brew. It was fine, hints of whiskey behind the dominant citrus, so it was probably barrel aged.

"I came to admit this foamy shit has a little flavor," Lee continued. "But I'd trade my truck for a case of Miller." He finished his pint with a belch. The bartender, an older, tall man with wire-rim glasses and tattoos on his fingers, immediately placed another down on a new napkin. He swiped away the empty glass.

"Probably aren't too many people who even remember Bud, Miller, Coors," Tom said, scratching his chin. He knew a man, a few men actually, who dealt in black-market beer. He knew a few others that brewed fake versions that tasted like dead mice and sawdust.

"It's maybe the one thing about this world I don't like," Lee said.

Tom heard one of the two men smoking in the front say something that sounded like "storm's coming." He looked over at them, their beards stained with nicotine.

"If that's true," Lee muttered, "you might be here in town for a few more days. A week maybe." Lee pulled another swallow. "These storms."

Tom knew what the man was thinking. "They were never this bad years ago."

Lee paused for a moment before replying. "You're a city boy, ain'tcha."

"Grand Rapids."

"Michigan or Minnesota?" Lee answered his own question. "Michigan, I reckon. I don't hear any Minnesota."

Tom nodded.

"How did you get out here then?"

Tom finished his pint.

"Shouldn't you be drinkin' vodka?" Lee asked, turning to look at Tom for the first time since they sat down. "Or scotch or some shit?"

Tom asked for another pint. He waited for the bartender to bring it. Lee went back to his own. When Tom received his beer, he took a swallow before beginning his answer. "When I was a kid, there weren't Indian tribes in lower Michigan. Except Sag Chip. Everyone was living in the city. Urban Indians."

"There were real Indians up here," Lee said loudly. He reached again for his pint. "Urban Indians, my ass," he muttered.

Tom didn't look over, but, in his mind's eye, he could see Lee roll his eyes at the mention of urban Indians. The fat man knew how to hit back. "When you were a kid, you ever go to the lodge at Bad River? Red Cliff?" Tom knew someone like Lee wouldn't have gone there. In the sheriff's formative years, and, in the eyes of the people that raised him, Indians were outcasts, losers, drunks, living off the government tit, stealing all the fish, going nowhere, waiting to die.

"I sure as shit know you didn't, either," Lee said. "City boy."

Tom didn't answer. It was true. He knew one Indian kid when he was growing up in GR in the 1970s. "Got a wart on your fanny, sheriff?"

"Naw." The big man took another deep drink and received another pint. He scratched his left arm and his neck. The DNA Indigenization treatment caused rashes, relentlessly itchy rashes, in some people. Some people died. But it was worth it for these white men. No one wanted to be an immigrant, or the son of an immigrant. This is America, they said, and we're Americans. The treatment started with the rich, lefty elites, a sort of joke to poke at the anti-immigrant people. It didn't take long for political elites in both parties to sign up. After a few years, you could buy it at Wal-Marts. A shitty version anyway.

Tom wondered how much longer the sheriff was going to survive the treatment. The older people got, the worse the complications. Skin rashes from the pigmentation changes and blindness from the change in eye color were survivable. The diabetes was not. The cancer was not.

"Just shootin' the shit's all." The big man was sweating. The wood stove in the back of the bar was starting to glow red. "Gonna be a long night's all."

Tom looked out the front window and saw more snow coming down. The wind was picking up.

It had been years since Tom had been inside a Midewewin lodge, or whatever one might call this stick house monstrosity full of anxious, pasty-faced, itchy white people. He did his best to not look around like a tourist, but he was checking it out. The doorkeeper at the eastern end looked he might be the only real Indian in the whole place. And that dude wasn't making eye contact with anyone there, holding his eagle staff like he wanted to stab someone with it, staring daggers at the other side of the door frame.

"Brother," Tom said to the doorkeeper as he entered in his moccasins, ducking under the maple sapling at the top end of the eastern door. Most everything Tom saw inside the lodge looked like what he had read about Mide. There were children gathered around elders, helping them put together what looked like a water drum. There were blankets all around the outside of the lodge where people sat working on a beading project. People were talking socially, laughing. It was a nice environment. "No wonder Indians liked this sort of thing back in the day," he mumbled. He sat down next to the doorkeeper.

"Where you from?" Tom asked. The question was the code for asking about someone's tribal identification. If the answer was a hometown, then Tom would know to think the respondent wasn't Indian.

"KB," the doorkeeper said, barely above a whisper but with gravel in his voice, staring straight ahead. The man wore faded jeans and red flannel. His moccasins were nice but no beads. He had acne scars but nothing like the skin disasters that filled the lodge. Short, jet black hair, Marine cut.

Keweenaw Bay Indian Community, Tom thought. He leaned into the doorkeeper and whispered. "So you're actually 'Nish? What are you doing here?"

The doorkeeper didn't answer for a time. Tom was about to move along when the man said, "This was my lodge."

Tom nodded. He scanned the lodge, and the larger barn that housed the lodge. He saw the familiar scratch marks on the older people, the splotchy skin and eczema on the younger kids. The older ones having undergone gene therapy years ago, their kids the issue of altered adults. The doorkeeper was interesting to Tom. "Why you still here?"

Finally, the doorkeeper turned to look at Tom, bitterness written all over his face. "You coming in? Or leaving?"

Tom stood and walked away from the doorkeeper. At least the man was doing his job, moving people along. He wandered along the sitting places to the left, moving in a clockwise direction like he had read about in old anthropology monographs describing the Midewewin religion. He stepped around an ancient, fat white lady splayed out on a Pendleton blanket with a Star Wars theme on it, trying but not quite figuring out how the lady was going to stand up again. The sage odor, cut with a healthy dose of sweetgrass and semaa, dominated the room. It got more intense as Tom approached the sacred fire in the middle. A pale man with a long red braid sat there tending the fire, tossing in scraps of tobacco, making the coals spark a little. The fire keeper was probably bored. "Aanii," Tom said, sitting down on a lawn chair next to the fire pit.

"Enh," the man said companionably. He half stood and reached back to scratch the top of his ass crack.

"Where you from?"

"The Cities."

Tom smiled. "Ah. Urban Indian, eh?"

The fire keeper looked confused. "What?"

Tom decided to try again. "What brings you out here?"

The man grunted. "I hated the Cities."

Tom knew that was code, too.

"I live here now. Have for . . . twenty-five years or so."

"You still have people back there?"

"Ehn. Don't need those people though." The derision in his voice. "These people are my people now."

Tom felt exiled from the urban areas and wanted to go back. This man had exiled himself and would never go back.

"Quit it," a woman shouted to a small child to Tom's left. He started and looked over. She backhanded the kid, who was maybe four, maybe five. The woman was mid-twenties, wearing a ratty T-shirt commemorating a black metal band Tom had never heard of, Okeus. Her arms were tattooed, which Tom knew was never a good thing for an altered white person with bad skin. It was apparent from the open sores on her arms she had been fighting, unsuccessfully, infection piled on top of infection. The kid was crying like he had never been hit before. Tom figured this kid was hit all the time, so it was an act, but still.

The fire keeper wasn't asking Tom to leave, so he settled down onto the lawn chair. He retrieved his leather notebook from his bag and opened it up. Lodge members weren't allowed books or writing instruments while in the lodge, but Tom suspected that certain men wouldn't be questioned. The doorkeeper. The fire keeper. The law keeper. He glanced around, saw no one looking at him sideways, and turned to his materials.

Tom could still smell the murderer's blood. He knew it could happen because he had seen amateur videos, or parts of them. The tribal snuff videos. He'd never make it to the kill shot, pausing the screen right after the sentence was handed down. He had seen it, but he had never once expected the murder of a murderer to be so brazen, right there in a Midewewin lodge, with dozens of onlookers. Kids running around playing tag. Old people beading and crocheting. The blood spray from the guy's neck shot fifteen feet forward, splashing into the coals of the sacred fire. Some of the blood hit Tom and the rest of the high-level Midewewin priests sitting near the fire pit. Tom was aghast. And so was pretty much everyone else in the lodge, the only thing that settled Tom's nerves. At least these people weren't complete savages.

Tom looked behind him to the doorkeeper, but he was gone, replaced by a young white man, altered like the rest of them.

"That's justice," Tom heard the fire keeper say with satisfaction, even as several others screamed and most of the members of the lodge scrambled to exit. "And right in front of the western door," the fire keeper added. "The right way. The old way." The man with the red braid and fresh blood dripping from his Viking beard looked over at Tom. "You really know what you're doing," the man said with veneration.

Tom said nothing. He gathered himself, controlled his emotions, and nodded back at the fire keeper. The lodge smelled a little like a burned steak to Tom. It reminded him of the good Kobe he ate regularly at expensive restaurants in Manhattan and Los Angeles when he was a young lawyer, when his clients were corporations engaged in complex litigation over hundreds of millions of dollars.

Once Tom realized he wasn't of any more use to the remaining members of the lodge—no one would expect a fourth-degree Mide priest to clean up blood and dispose of a human body—he quietly exited. He was a law keeper, but an outsider. He wouldn't be expected to stay at the lodge anyway. Tom drove his truck on the two-lane blacktop cradled by snow on either side of the road, anxious for a drink. Booze was the best thing left about the closed-off rural areas of the Great Lakes. Distilleries and microbreweries tended to operate freely in the rural areas, few people around to be bothered by the odors. Of course, the beef was good, too, but Tom thought that his taste for red meat might be gone for a long time after that day. It was a fifteen-mile trip back to town.

The doorkeeper with the Marine cut was sitting at the bar of the small restaurant in the hotel. The restaurant was pretty rundown. But it had the postindustrial decor popular with resort rural establishments and outdoor gear shops, from the decade or so before the split from the cities. Time and lack of proper maintenance made most of the metal fixtures look rusty. The furniture broke down long ago and was replaced with discarded odds and ends from the chain restaurants that didn't survive long past the break. The concrete floor hadn't been sealed in a long time.

"Anishinaabe na gidow," Tom said, lifting his leg over the bar stool closest to the doorkeeper.

The doorkeeper was nursing a black coffee. "You know I am," he said without humor.

"I thought Indians had a good sense of humor," Tom said to the doorkeeper. He asked the bartender for a local IPA.

"Something smells funny," the doorkeeper said dryly.

Tom laughed, a little unhealthy squeak he had never heard himself make before. "Yeah, I ought to change." He looked down at the blood on his jeans and shoes.

"They having a barbecue over at the lodge?" the doorkeeper asked.

Tom looked over at the man, who was staring straight ahead.

"Smells like meat." He said it with an emphasis on the "t" sound.

Tom excused himself to change. He did so quickly, hoping to rejoin the doorkeeper before the man left. He was pleased to see the man hadn't moved. He sat down again and finally asked the man his name.

"Wesaw."

"Wesaw. If I recall correctly, that's a Potawatomi name."

"Yep."

Tom knew the next question was fraught. "Pokagon?"

Wesaw smirked. "Everyone asks that."

"Yes," Tom said. "Everyone wants to be a son of Leopold."

"I am a Pokagon descendant."

Tom was impressed. "That's really something."

"Leopold to Alexander to Peter to Laura to Junior."

Doubly impressed. "Wow. You're the real deal, eh?"

"Sure I am," Wesaw said, monotone-like, pretending to be unconvincing.

"A simple DNA test . . ."

"Hell." Barely a whisper.

Tom smiled. He liked this guy. He took a sip of the beer, now getting warm. But Wesaw was right. He had no business bothering the doorkeeper with an interrogation. He sat still and looked ahead.

After a time. "What's your story, white man?"

Tom knew he would have to tell a story about himself to get into this man's mind. But he didn't know what story. He didn't know what he had in his own mind that was worth telling. "I used to drink the good scotch. The single malt, fifteen years, eighteen years, double cask. Peaty. Like drinking straight out of a camp fire." It was a beginning.

"And now you drink craft beer," Wesaw said. He wanted to hear more. "And sentence men to die."

"Is that what I did?" Tom asked, trying—but not really trying—to sound concerned. "I thought I did the opposite."

"What did you do?" Wesaw had left the lodge before the trial commenced, turning his duties over to an apprentice just after Tom asked the men to conduct the tobacco ceremony.

Tom told Wesaw about the murderer's family, who begged from their side of the lodge for the life of their relation. The murderer was a nineteen-year-old kid with a good family, who ran with a bad crowd. His mother described how the murderer, a boy really, had taken to drinking with these bad kids, staying out late. The victim was one of those bad kids. The murderer's mom blamed the bad kids and the bad family, the same family that sat across from the mom while she spoke and wept to save her son. Tom suspected the ogemaag weren't buying her story. The victim's family wasn't, either, though they were polite enough to listen without betraying their anger openly. The rest of the lodge members seemed anxious, but Tom didn't know why. Not then. Not right away. "I described how every life in a tribal community has value," Tom said.

"Every person has something important to contribute. Every individual is indispensable. I gave the teaching of the tobacco ceremony. We all shared the pipe. We are one community."

"They, you mean," Wesaw said. "You and me. We're outsiders. We don't belong there."

Tom nodded, though he still wondered why Wesaw had anything at all to do with this lodge. Or why Wesaw was staying in a tourists' hotel fifteen miles away.

"You did the thing where you gave the killer to the victim's family, right?" Wesaw asked. He finished his coffee and motioned for another.

Tom nodded again, looking over at Wesaw. Wesaw knew the stories, the ceremonies, the history. Why wasn't he the leader of the lodge?

"What I bet you don't know is that this has happened before here," Wesaw said. "The kid's mother wasn't asking *you* to spare his son. She was asking the other family. She knew her judge, I think. She knew you were an outsider. She believed you would never banish the boy. Or have the boy killed. You'd think you were being merciful. And do exactly what you did."

The killer stood up from the center of the lodge when Tom stated the judgment. He went over to his family, weeping, hugging, kissing, being kissed, saying goodbye, a dozen baamaapii-s. The victim's family stood as one. Tom didn't see the long knife the oldest member of the victim's family was hiding. As soon as the killer reached the blankets of his new family, the victim's father slashed the kid across the throat.

"Though I've never seen them kill the killer right there in the lodge in front of everybody," Wesaw said. "It's getting bad in this lodge. Hell, it's always been bad in this lodge."

Tom rubbed his chin. It was getting worse everywhere he went.

Thinking about What I've Done

I remember Emily Gordon sitting in the corner on a little red plastic chair thinking about what she had done. She had straight black hair, a round face, and high cheekbones. A perfect little Indian girl. I felt sorry for her, but I also wanted to be better than her.

Our teacher, a grown man who wanted us to call him The Ape, didn't make her face the wall. No, she had to sit and watch all the other kids play, play and be socialized. Considering the amount of time Emily sat in the corner, it was a wonder she ever learned to function in the world at all.

Emily was the smartest girl in my class from kindergarten at Steeby Elementary until graduation from our dilapidated high school. And in kindergarten and first grade, she was the best of all of us. She was shocking and boisterous. She made us laugh, knocked us down to size, and made us feel like little royals. Her mom tied her hair up in a ponytail, and it would bob up and down from the top of her skull. She told us in kindergarten that her mom and dad were Indians, and so she was an Indian, too. My mom and I were Indians, too—Potawatomis. But Emily would change over time, and she would stop wearing the ponytail. In fifth grade, she would tell us she was an *Ottawa Indian*. In seventh grade, she became *Odawa*. And not an Indian, a *Native American*. In tenth grade, she went back to being an Ottawa, but by then she was a *Grand Traverse Band Ottawa*. By the time we graduated from Wayland Union High in 1990, she sometimes referred to herself as an *Anishinaabe*, but, since no one ever heard of that, she settled for Ottawa again. And at Lisa Candelaria's high school graduation party, I thought I heard her say she was *Anishinaabekwe*—an Anishinaabe woman.

We were never close friends. I should say we were never friends at all. In kindergarten, everyone in class was a friend, before first grade socialization kicked in and created outcasts and cliques. And like everyone who had a birthday party in first grade, I invited Emily. We didn't play much together and we weren't neighbors, but she was fun. I invited half the first grade class—all the boys, a couple girls that lived on my street, and Emily. Everyone showed up, except Emily. I didn't even notice until two decades later when my mother brought out old photos from the basement, looking for pictures of a long lost relative. I can see the old house on Forrest Street, the inside ripped to shreds by two hours of birthday party madness. We were all gathered around for a group picture, everyone getting ready to leave. No Emily.

I mean, I understand it was first grade. I'm sure no slight was intended. Emily got invited to every party. She couldn't go to all of them. And it's not like she had a car or a chauffeur to drive her around on her various social appointments. Maybe the invitation my mom sent to her house never arrived. Maybe my mom wrote the wrong address.

In second grade, The Ape kept sending Emily to the corner to think about what she had done. I remember The Ape putting on his ape mask the first time and making us laugh with his monkey shines. I remember how he used to make us laugh just as Emily had made us laugh in kindergarten and first grade. But when the bell rang, he demanded obedience and quiet. He told us it was what we would need to do in the real world. And when he sent Emily to the corner for mouthing off or laughing too loud, he would leave her there a long time. She was a bright, thoughtful girl, so she must have done a whole lot of thinking. Some days, she might have spent two or three hours in the corner. Some days, she forfeited recess. Some days, she had to eat cold lunch and drink white milk with The Ape in our cold classroom while the rest of us ate hot lunches and drank chocolate milk in the gym.

Our kindergarten teacher, Mr. Tom, had informed my parents that I was a slow Indian and wouldn't graduate from high school. I proved him wrong, but it took me until second grade to show my chops. The Ape allowed us to work in our spelling books at our own pace. The spelling workbook was a big, oily bastard that took most of the kids in class until December to finish. I finished in early October. Emily, sitting mostly in the corner with no desk, finished two weeks behind me. I was teacher's pet to The Ape. He asked me to write the weekly spelling tests he offered to the other students. He asked me to craft crossword puzzles using that week's vocabulary words for the other kids to solve, including Emily. I wonder if she resented me, if she was jealous of my special place in class. I wrote out in longhand the rudimentary spelling tests and assignment sheets. I even delivered the afternoon milk tray from the kitchen. Had I been ten or fifteen years older, The Ape would have sent me to pick up his dry cleaning and buy his cigarettes from the gas station by the VFW. While I was hustling for The Ape after finishing my workbook, Emily sat in the corner doing nothing but thinking about what she had done.

Everyone considered me the smartest kid as we entered the third grade. Dondi, my best remaining friend from school, once admitted to me I intimidated everyone in third grade. He said I ruled the class with an iron fist. I responded that Larry Barnett, the ten-year-old, 120-pound, third-grade delinquent used to scare the hell out of me and everyone else, but Dondi shook his head. I remembered wrong, he said. Even Larry followed my lead. Dondi said that, in fact, Larry was only the third most intimidating kid in class—Emily had Larry beat out, too.

I remember little about her in third grade. She was no longer boisterous, and, since I was the smartest and she was a *girl*, Emily was no longer worthy of my attention. The Ape, the corner, and all that thinking about what she had done fixed her but good, as they say. It must have been that year where she acquired that superior, persecuted air. I lost track of her.

In third grade, R. J. Steeby still used textbooks copyrighted in 1972, the year I was born, a fact I thought was cool. My mom, who commuted to Grand Rapids every day for work, didn't think that was very cool and had the bright idea to enroll me in the new gifted and talented program in the GR public schools. One day a week, I would wake up at 5 a.m., ride with my mom to the city, and attend this special school for gifted kids. (Not necessarily "smart," mind you, but "gifted"; "smart" being an abstract word based on the IQ test that could no longer be considered an objective indicator. Lots of kids were "smart," *see* Emily, but not everyone was "gifted.") Getting the school district's permission to take me out of school for a day a week was my mother's second foray into confronting that esteemed board of elected white people (more on the first later). She explained that Wayland and its eighteenth-century teaching methods would stunt my intellectual growth, and so on.

It seemed that I was so smart by the beginning of fourth grade that they couldn't even keep me in class. Of course, not being in class made it more difficult to maintain good grades, the objective indicators of my intelligence, those letter grades we had all heard about but hadn't seen on our report cards until fourth grade. I struggled to maintain Bs at Steeby school. And in the gifted and talented program, I wasn't the smartest. I wasn't the dumbest either (a short kid named Dustan took that honor; he wore a winter coat indoors and swore up and down that he remembered the moment of his birth), but I wasn't used to putting forth effort. And city kids were worldly, like those kids always getting in trouble on afterschool specials. We Wayland kids (e.g., me) were more like the farm animals on *Green Acres*. I did the Tuesday gifted and talented thing for two years until my parents yanked me out and told me to go back to being the kid I was in second and third grades.

By the beginning of sixth grade, I had become a cult figure, almost a ghost of my former self. After the experience of going to school once a week with the afterschool-special kids, I thought Steeby Elementary was a big, fat joke. And to be fair, my teachers thought I was a big, fat joke, too. They hadn't seen my brilliance at that spelling workbook in second grade or how I dominated the room with my wit and charisma in third grade. I was in danger of becoming one of those Indian kids who starts smoking in sixth grade, drinking in seventh grade, skipping too much school in junior high, and sniffing glue or huffing gas in ninth grade. Selling pot from Hefty bags and cooking meth from my dad's barn was next and then, because of I'm Indian, probably juvie and then prison.

Sixth grade just about did me in. Twelve-year-olds are pure evil. I got called fat, ugly, stupid, and retarded more that year than any other year before or since—combined. No one would have considered a boy the smartest anything (except maybe smartest ass) by the end of that year. The girls hit puberty, and they knew the answer to every question. Boys were loud, and, though years away from realizing that they were from

Mars, they went to Jupiter, where they went to get more stupider. The smartest boys were always dumber than all the girls. The dumb boys, however, acquired popularity while nerds and dorks appeared out of nowhere like termites.

But for six weeks at the beginning of sixth grade, the old me was back. It was our teacher. A regular teacher would have bored me to death and driven me to my mom's cigarettes. A bad teacher could have done worse. But our teacher—later memorialized as The Drunk—was awesome. I was the smartest kid. School was fun again. Well, to be fair, our egalitarian Drunk implied that five of us were the smartest. Me, Emily, Dondi, Lisa Candelaria, and a kid who moved away in December named Ridge. It felt good to be king again—it felt right—and I blew the fifty bucks my dad gave me for my good grades on baseball cards.

It didn't last. The Drunk was an alcoholic. He stopped coming to work, and we started seeing more and more of another teacher. She became our full-time teacher by Halloween. That teacher was a very, very bad teacher. I went from being the smartest kid to the most disappointing. Dondi went from being the smartest to being an overachieving jock with no future. Lisa went from being the smartest to being the spoiled brat daughter of the town mayor. Ridge went from being the smartest to living in Alaska.

And Emily went from being the smartest kid to being the biggest, most heinous bitch in the history of Allegan County.

We knew these things because our new permanent substitute teacher told us all these things in private conferences. She started to tell us all off.

So I stopped being the smartest kid again in sixth grade. I did OK in junior high. I'd pick up a few As on every report card, but I didn't do as well as my test scores suggested I should. In eighth grade, they placed me in Wayland's first gifted and talented class. My mom did a third bit of wrangling with the school board over that one, the board arguing that my grades and my failure in the Grand Rapids program counseled against trying me out again. But my mom was crafty. Whatever she did, it worked. It always worked.

I expected to see Emily (the smartest), Lisa, maybe Dondi, and a few others in my class, but I didn't see any of them. Somehow, "smartest" and "gifted" had become mutually exclusive at Wayland.

So my "gifted" class and I learned about Dante and Shakespeare and Elizabeth Barrett Browning and plagiarism, but I wondered what the smart people were doing while we watched *West Side Story*. The rest of the kids in my gifted class would never populate the top of the honor roll then or later in high school.

And then, near the end of eighth grade, my gifted class teacher's film student daughter turned the goofy little screenplay I wrote for class into a short film. It was a rewriting of *Beowulf* involving smart, elitist kids, who triumph over dumb, mean kids and their mothers. The director premiered the film in the Ann Arbor film festival. That same summer a literary magazine published by a community college English department published a poem I wrote about despair in middle school. Armed with two pieces of art, I turned into a small-town rock star. Even the stoners compared me to the guy from Middleville who became the bassist for Metallica.

My artistic well dried up after that, but the high school assistant principal still gave me a special plaque for proving that not all Wayland students are lifeless bags of flesh. I read my poem, and they showed my film in front of the entire school at an assembly at the beginning of ninth grade. The football players and the girls' basketball team remembered the film, and the suicides and the forensics team remembered the poem.

Once I became known as a screenwriter and poet, I returned to the throne of the school. I didn't have to do much to keep my title ("the smartest"). I took a lot of B-plusses and A-minuses, but I always carried around a battered copy of *Ulysses* or *The Waste Land* for effect. I carried one or the other around in law school, too, when I realized there was no difference between law school and high school—lockers, cliques, bad drunken sex, teary melodrama, sack lunches, bulimia.

I took the prize away from Emily even though she never took less than a 95 percent on a test, never once took an A-minus on her report card. I suppose Emily didn't care. She thought she was above high school. She was a beautiful young woman and attended all the cool kids' parties with her special brand of condescension. She had her snooty nose up in the air while she passed the time before she became an important and powerful adult. And she would drink too much peach schnapps at parties (she was an angry drunk). Though I never witnessed an outburst from her, I heard about them from others. Flying off the handle over some perceived slight, she'd tell everyone around her that they were nobodies.

But Emily was still a teenager and—as afterschool specials taught us—teenagers make bad choices. She fell in love with a football player. She spent her time with people who made her feel fat and ugly. She obsessed over bad television dramas about wealthy white people. The biggest mistake was the football player. She did more for him that he did for her. He took all the college-prep classes to be near her, and he actually did okay, well enough to go to a decent college. She taught him to think like an adult and to stop smoking. In return, he drafted a list of ten pretty girls he wanted to fuck by the time he graduated. Emily was number two on the list. Her older sister, a Grand Valley State undergraduate, was number one. By the time Emily discovered the list, eight names had been crossed off. Only Emily's sister and Lisa Candelaria remained untouched.

I don't recall ever conversing with Emily in high school. I might have said, "Excuse me" when I nearly spilled a beaker of partially diluted sulfuric acid on her new shoes once, but we never talked. We never said hello in the morning or nodded to each other as an acknowledgment of the other's brilliance or Anishinaabe confederacy. As far as I can tell, there was no jealousy or hatred between us other than the nonspecific hatred toward all of us that emanated from Emily like an odor.

The next time I saw Emily after high school graduation and graduation parties, I was a third-year law student, confident and laid-back about my future career and life as an Indian lawyer. I had just left Immigration and Refugee Asylum Law and entered the hallway. It was packed, as usual, for the time of day, with first-year law students leaving Kamisar's criminal law shouting match. I usually slipped out the back door to avoid people, but I was supposed to meet a friend on the other end of the building for lunch. So I pushed against the grain of 1Ls. I muddled through and looked up to see Emily standing right in front of me. She looked the same but tougher, meaner—a first-year law student. Law school must have made her put up the defenses even stronger than usual. She saw me, too, and she must have recognized me. She stared me dead in the eye and paused for just a moment. The shock of seeing each other. I blinked first, and in that instant she moved on, elbowing right past me. It was high school all over again. She didn't need to acknowledge me, speak to me, or catch up with me. We were nothing to each other.

We should have become great friends, compatriots, allies, something—two Anishinaabes, same lousy public school district, kindergarten through twelfth grade. We both got out of there and succeeded. We were both going to be lawyers, graduates of the finest, most prestigious law school in Michigan. We should have relied on each other for advice and counsel because we understood each other's past better than no one else.

But none of that happened.

I didn't see Emily again in law school. And then I graduated and moved out west. Sometimes I tell my friends the story about how I saw a woman from Wayland in Hutchins Hall and that she was Indian, too. I also tell them how she wouldn't talk to me in the hallway, leaving out the part about how I didn't talk to her, either. My friends say that law school sometimes changes people and maybe she just turned into a bad apple. I say I couldn't disagree because I knew her from the beginning of grade school. But I also knew about her struggles against The Ape and the football player. And she knew about my struggles to be a "gifted" student, how I was a disappointment and an underachiever. We both survived our sixth-grade substitute teacher. We both survived being Indian in a white, rural school district, with its attendant racism and sexism and other assorted bigotries.

But we had never relied on each other. I realize that we had always been rivals and would never be friends. The law school brush-off was the same brush-off we had been giving each other for twenty years. I think about all the times I saw Emily at powwows and camp meetings in Grand Rapids, Dowagiac, White Pigeon, and Mount Pleasant when we were kids. We never talked. We saw each other and walked the other way. We always had. I don't remember a conversation with her. Ever. Not one.

It's been ten years since I last saw Emily in that hallway in Hutchins Hall, and I haven't seen her since. I've been working in Indian law for those years, and I've met a hundred Indian lawyers in that time. I've heard stories about a couple hundred more. It seems everyone who works in Indian Country knows everyone else. It's an insular community. You could fit all the Indian law practitioners and academics into one big corporate law firm and still have room for a large mergers and acquisitions or international finance practice group. There just aren't very many.

And Emily isn't one of us.

I imagine Emily did what most of our colleagues at Michigan Law would go on to do—work for a corporate law firm or a corporation or the federal government or maybe become a law professor. That's what the law school wanted us to do. It was the method the school used to ensure that the alumni contributions would keep coming in and maintain the school's prestige. The law school counselors were willing to help me find a job in Seattle working for Berkman, Deloria, Goldman, and Petoskey or the Environmental Protection Agency, but they didn't help me find a job as in-house counsel for an Indian tribe. Maybe the same was true for Emily.

In my first job for a tribe in Arizona, I got paid about $30,000 a year. Not bad money, but the real benefit for me was working at a place where most of the other employees were Indians. There were Navajos and Apaches and O'odham and Yaquis and Pomo Indians. My first major project in Arizona was going to the local school board to ask them to change their history textbooks to books that wrote about the local Indians in a better light than repeated references to the word "savage." It reminded me of my mother's first foray before the Wayland school board, demanding the same thing in 1981. The school board told me to get lost, but it was satisfying to try.

In Emily's first job, assuming she received the average job for a Michigan Law graduate in 1999, she would have been paid about $110,000 and worked in Manhattan, DC, Chicago, or San Francisco. She would have been the lone Indian working at a big firm with over one hundred or five hundred or two thousand lawyers. She would be the token Indian. And when she went out with her friends at night, she'd be the only Indian in the group, the only Indian in the bar or restaurant. It would be just like law school. But maybe that's what she would want. Maybe she craved the uniqueness of being the only Indian in her social group. Maybe she could still be a Grand Traverse Band Ottawa and a lawyer for a big corporate firm with non-Indians for clients.

I've been thinking about what I've done, and I can't come up with any answers. I don't know why we weren't friends. I don't know why we ignored each other as though we were ashamed of ourselves. I don't know why I was the smartest kid in high school and not her. I don't know why I keep thinking about her.

And I don't know what I will say to Emily if I ever see her again.

Acknowledgments

"Truck Stop" was originally published in *UMKC Law Review* 76, no. 3 (Spring 2008).

"Knuckle-Curve" was originally published in *NINE: A Journal of Baseball History and Culture* 14, no. 2 (Spring 2006).

"Badder Road" was originally published in the *Dunes Review: Literary Journal of Northwestern Lower Michigan* 9, no. 2 (Winter 2004).

"The Chain Gangs" was originally published in *Terraspatial: Scissor Press Online Zine* (2002).

"An Iranian in de Gaulle" was originally published in *Snow Monkey: An Eclectic Journal* 5, no. 3 (2003).

"The Village by the Sea" was originally published in the *Dunes Review: Literary Journal of Northwestern Lower Michigan* 8, no. 1 (Summer 2003).

"Ten-Year Visit" was originally published in *Znine: Online Literary Review of the University of Texas at Arlington* (Spring 2004).

"Thinking about What I've Done" was originally published in *Red Ink* 13, no. 2 (Fall 2007).

Aazheyaadizi: *Worldview, Language, and the Logics of Decolonization*, Mark D. Freeland | 978-1-61186-380-2

As Sacred to Us: Simon Pokagon's Birch Bark Stories in Their Contexts, edited by Blaire Morseau | 978-1-61186-462-5

Bawaajimo*: A Dialect of Dreams in Anishinaabe Language and Literature*, Margaret Noodin | 978-1-61186-105-1

Centering Anishinaabeg Studies: Understanding the World through Stories, edited by Jill Doerfler, Niigaanwewidam James Sinclair, and Heidi Kiiwetinepinesiik Stark | 978-1-61186-067-2

Curator of Ephemera at the New Museum for Archaic Media, Heid E. Erdrich | 978-1-61186-246-1

Document of Expectations, Devon Abbott Mihesuah | 978-1-61186-011-5

Dragonfly Dance, Denise K. Lajimodiere | 978-0-87013-982-6

Encountering the Sovereign Other: Indigenous Science Fiction, Miriam C. Brown Spiers | 978-1-61186-405-2

Facing the Future: The Indian Child Welfare Act at 30, edited by Matthew L. M. Fletcher, Wenona T. Singel, and Kathryn E. Fort | 978-0-87013-860-7

Famine Pots: The Choctaw–Irish Gift Exchange, 1847–Present, edited by LeAnne Howe and Padraig Kirwan | 978-1-61186-369-7

Follow the Blackbirds, Gwen Nell Westerman | 978-1-61186-092-4

Gambling on Authenticity: Gaming, the Noble Savage, and the Not-So-New Indian, edited by Becca Gercken and Julie Pelletier | 978-1-61186-256-0

Indian Country: Telling a Story in a Digital Age, Victoria L. LaPoe and Benjamin Rex LaPoe II | 978-1-61186-226-3

The Indian Who Bombed Berlin and Other Stories, Ralph Salisbury | 978-0-87013-847-8

Indigenizing Philosophy through the Land: A Trickster Methodology for Decolonizing Environmental Ethics and Indigenous Futures, Brian Burkhart | 978-1-61186-330-7

Indigenous Journeys, Transatlantic Perspectives: Relational Worlds in Contemporary Native American Literature, Anna M. Brígido-Corachán | 978-1-61186-469-4

Indigenous Poetics, edited by Inés Hernández-Ávila and Molly McGlennen | 978-1-61186-526-4

Louise Erdrich's Justice Trilogy: Cultural and Critical Contexts, edited by Connie A. Jacobs and Nancy J. Peterson | 978-1-61186-403-8

Masculindians: Conversations about Indigenous Manhood, edited by Sam McKegney | 978-1-61186-129-7

Mediating Indianness, edited by Cathy Covell Waegner | 978-1-61186-151-8

The Murder of Joe White: Ojibwe Leadership and Colonialism in Wisconsin, Erik M. Redix | 978-1-61186-145-7

National Monuments, Heid E. Erdrich | 978-0-87013-848-5

Ogimawkwe Mitigwaki (Queen of the Woods), Simon Pokagon | 978-0-87013-987-1

Ottawa Stories from the Springs: Anishinaabe dibaadjimowinan wodi gaa binjibaamigak wodi mookodjiwong e zhinikaadek, translated and edited by Howard Webkamigad | 978-1-61186-137-2

Picturing Worlds: Visuality and Visual Sovereignty in Contemporary Anishinaabe Literature, David Stirrup | 978-1-61186-352-9

Plain of Jars and Other Stories, Geary Hobson | 978-0-87013-998-7

Sacred Wilderness, Susan Power | 978-1-61186-111-2

Seeing Red—Hollywood's Pixeled Skins: American Indians and Film, edited by LeAnne Howe, Harvey Markowitz, and Denise K. Cummings | 978-1-61186-081-8

Self-Determined Stories: The Indigenous Reinvention of Young Adult Literature, Mandy Suhr-Sytsma | 978-1-61186-298-0

Shedding Skins: Four Sioux Poets, edited by Adrian C. Louis | 978-0-87013-823-2

Sounding Thunder: The Stories of Francis Pegahmagabow, Brian D. McInnes | 978-1-61186-225-6

Stick Houses: Stories, Matthew L. M. Fletcher | 978-1-61186-522-6

Stories for a Lost Child, Carter Meland | 978-1-61186-244-7

Stories through Theories/Theories through Stories: North American Indian Writing, Storytelling, and Critique, edited by Gordon D. Henry Jr., Nieves Pascual Soler, and Silvia Martinez-Falquina | 978-0-87013-841-6

That Guy Wolf Dancing, Elizabeth Cook-Lynn | 978-1-61186-138-9

Those Who Belong: Identity, Family, Blood, and Citizenship among the White Earth Anishinaabeg, Jill Doerfler | 978-1-61186-169-3

Visualities: Perspectives on Contemporary American Indian Film and Art, edited by Denise K. Cummings | 978-0-87013-999-4

Visualities 2: More Perspectives on Contemporary American Indian Film and Art, edited by Denise K. Cummings | 978-1-61186-319-2

Writing Home: Indigenous Narratives of Resistance, Michael D. Wilson | 978-0-87013-818-8